the way of the lightkeeper

YOUR INNER PATHWAY
TO SPIRITUAL LIBERATION

catherine grace landry

http://www.satiamapublishing.com

The Way of the Lightkeeper

By Catherine Grace Landry

Copyright 2019, Catherine Grace Landry and
Satiama Publishing

Published and distributed by Satiama Publishing, a service
mark of Satiama, LLC

(www.satiamapublishing.com)

PO Box 1397
Palmer Lake, CO 80133
719-487-0424

E-book: 978-0-9972825-5-9
Softcover book: 978-0-9972825-4-2

Library of Congress Cataloging-in-Publication Number
2019953587

1. New Thought 2. Inspiration and Personal Growth
3. Personal Development

Written by Catherine Grace Landry
Graphic design by Julia McMinn Evans
Copyright 2019, Catherine Grace Landry and
Satiama Publishing

The intent of the author and artist is only to offer information of a general nature to help you in your quest for emotional and spiritual well-being. In the event you use any of the information in this book for yourself, which is your constitutional right, the authors and the publisher assume no responsibility for your actions.

For more information about Catherine Grace Landry, visit catherinegracelandry.com.

For more information about Satiama Publishing, visit satiamapublishing.com.

PRINTED IN CHINA

1 2 3 4 5 6 7 8 9 10

The Way of the Lightkeeper

I am that child

I am wonder

I am joy

I am compassion

I hold integrity and impeccability in the palms of
my hands as I reach out to you

The time is always present

The space is always Light

Be at peace…be content…be filled

The loop is always here...latch on!

I am. All that.

I am all that.

When I become what I am, there will be peace

When I open to the grace of my soul, there will I
have peace

I am grace.

I am a Keeper of the Light.

For R

And all the Lightkeepers of this world … and
beyond.

Contents

It is the darkest hour of the night.

The sky is an impenetrable black shield.

An inky velvet curtain veils the stars.

Neither creature nor plant dares challenge the endless chasm.

There is a silence so intense it is audible.

At the precise moment of profound stillness, an eerie wail erupts from the void with an electric urgency that penetrates all directions and dimensions.

It is that one unique sound that instantly captures the attention of all beings on this planet and beyond.

A human is born.

It is the moment of announcement, of heralding, of excitement beyond measure.

A Soul has successfully transited through layers of space and time, leaving its etheric home and slipping into the density of Earthly matter.

Its cry informs all that it has safely arrived and is ready to begin its newest journey.

It calls urgently to the Universe, and the Universe responds with delight.

1

A Time of Great Joy

The Spirit realms rejoice when a Soul completes its voyage to human form. The newborn also acutely feels this joy. Though the baby forgets its origins as it transits into human life, he or she can still experience the joy of the Universe, heralding its arrival. This joy carries the frequency of hope for the Soul now on its journey of remembering as a new baby births a new Light into the world. Its Light is pure, innocent, and untouched, and signals a fresh opportunity to transcend the ever-turning wheel of age-old pattern—the spiraling essence of our being.

My dream-vision of a baby's birth was one in a series of visions I recently received that were all delightful, odd, and seemingly unconnected. I am a grandmother well past the age of procreation. My dream-visions offered Medicine Men on mesa tops, knights of old, people and places unknown, panthers, and dinosaurs! Then they stopped. Curious, I randomly laid my journal notes for each vision on the floor and stood looking at them.

How strange, how fascinating, how bizarre!

Gradually I sensed a theme. Or perhaps it was a puzzle. The vision notes drew me into their midst until I was standing inside the circle of paper. They radiated all around me, each as important as the next, no beginning or ending, no hierarchy or structure. I began to feel dizzy and disoriented. The room started whirling around me, and I lost touch with my human senses.

I found myself swirling through a vortex out beyond this time and dimension, to a place of no-place where all was a field of colored lights and sounds that coalesced and separated as if by some unseen hand. Within this field, the dream-visions were moving fluidly in a dance orchestrated outside my comprehension. One or two would fuse, then separate; several would clump and then drift apart. This went on for what seemed like quite a while but was only a few moments of Earth time.

As my mind tried to make logical sense of what I was experiencing, I was flung back into my body to stand blinking in the daylight. Is this what our Soul experiences when it is born into human form? Little eyes blinking in the light, marveling at the sounds and colors that had yet to form into comprehensible shapes. This odd handful of dream-visions did gradually coalesce within my logical mind to a pattern; more like a kaleidoscope of patterns. Non-linear. Circular. Spiral. Points of a starburst. The patterns of our Light.

We are in a time of great expansion.

New pathways are lighting up within each of us. We are expanding in intelligence, awareness, knowledge. We are growing our capacity to love, to feel, to sense, to connect to all, to rediscover intuitive abilities at a rate exponentially faster than any time before. On a global scale, we perceive the need for impeccability of behavior and integrity of intention. We are awakening to the requirement to shift our traditional perspectives.

We are transcending our primal instincts that focus solely on survival. We are embracing a broader view of our 'selves' within a broader view of our human context. Our internal-facing compass is shifting to see both inwardly and outwardly. We are called to recalibrate all areas of our lives, and our societies to new, harmonious perspectives.

We are coming to the unshakeable realization

that the forces that created our world did so from love. We are opening up to what love truly means, and what we are required to do with this knowledge. Every aspect of life on our planet is being examined under a microscope of respect. We are redefining how we understand that word and how we act upon that concept.

We are coming to understand the true definition of liberty—that not one of us is actually free until we are all free. There can be no lasting joy should even one person still be enslaved, whether physically, emotionally, mentally, or spiritually. We are witness to movements across the globe of people rising up to break free from thoughts, beliefs, behaviors, and cultural patterns that no longer serve us or our planet.

We are bringing up to the light all long-buried darkness in our beliefs and actions, to understand, take responsibility, and release. We are simultaneously molding a new way of managing our interpersonal relations and our societies.

We are coming of age to a new era of universal

understanding of the concepts of love, freedom, joy. In this modern age, we are gifted with fresh energies propelling the momentum of expansion; the expansion of our ability to love, our ability to think, our ability to balance, our ability to see beyond these three dimensions. The expansion of our understanding of who and what we are, and who and what makes up our Universe and beyond.

We cannot fathom our full potential at this moment. We don't fully know, nor are we able to embrace all that we indeed are, but we are receiving glimpses of that expansive potential manifest in all of Creation, and this same potential in our own creations.

As we navigate these new pathways, we are compelled to seek more urgently that elusive something which calls us home to our Self. Who among us has not wished, pleaded at times, to feel a constant unshakeable force within our Self that never strays from our truest knowing? Who has not desired, at some time, to flow steadily with all the elements around us, to have them work through us and within us, to mold our bodies, flirt with our minds, and fire up our passions, yet never mis-step, mis-take, mis-use what and who we are.

There is such a force within each of us. Our body is but cells and systems and electrical currents functioning on certain principles. What animates this lump of carbon/hydrogen/nitrogen/oxygen is that which we have called through all the ages of this world the Light.

This series of dream-visions gifted me a fabulous phantasmagoria of information about this beautiful, mysterious, other-worldly force. Those dreams were grounded in actionable practicality for living in heart-centered joy in this complex maze of a world.

As the newborn opens its eyes and gradually focuses its thoughts to pull meaning and relevance out of the kaleidoscope of images dancing around it, so we are called to look upon this new era with the same curiosity. We are being asked to engage our child within and believe that there is still much to discover. We are all on this course together and it is changing each of us. There are no exceptions.

I dreamed of a black panther. Sleek and dark and powerful.

She padded towards me, gazing intently with unblinking green eyes straight into mine. She was compelling me to give in to her, to submit to her. I struggled. She waited patiently. She radiated an intensity I had never experienced before, as well as a unique frequency that piqued my curiosity. I gave in and accepted her lead. She pivoted and flicked her tail in command. With much trepidation, I followed.

It seemed we spun downwards through a never-ending tunnel of blackness. Hazy forms leaped from the shadows as we passed. These forms emanated anger. They did not want me in this place; they were trying to scare me into retreating, to prevent me from getting to our destination. Panther merely lifted a paw and swiped them away.

I had a strange sensation there was a Shining One—a Being of Light—trailing us, but my body seemed locked in a forward position, and I could not turn to investigate. It, too, was shattering the darkness around us with its Light to forge a safe passage.

Finally, we arrived in an open space. Panther drifted off to one side, curled up in a sleepy ball and waited, as if to say, "I got you here; now it is up to you."

Gingerly I looked around. I was in a cavernous space, perhaps a cave. I could not clearly discern the walls or roof. In the center, there was fire—a blazing, shining ring of flames.

I crept closer and saw that the ring of fire was actually a circle of Shining Ones. Not fire at all, but the brilliant Light emanating from these beings of the

Illumined realms. At the center was a baby, sleeping peacefully, protected by the circle of Light.

The Shining Ones moved aside and ushered me in. I asked the baby to wake. It joyfully opened its eyes and melted into my arms. I enfolded it within myself and promised to care for it. I asked, "What was this baby?" They told me it was my essence— the essence of Joy and Light.

2

Look Out Earth, Here We Come!

And so …. we are here.

We burst forth into the world with a mighty push, a watery gush, a colossal wriggling, and announced our presence with a hollering powerful enough to shake the very foundations of the planet. We signaled the Universe that we had arrived with the full power of our Soul and the greatest 'drama queen' performance of our life. We had made the journey intact. The Shining Ones sang their love and encouragement to us.

In my dream-visions, there are beings of luminescent white and rainbow colors that are clearly from a dimension other than ours, which I know as Shining Ones. Some might call them angels, elder guardians, spirits. However, we may label them, they are messengers of Light. They help us begin our Earthly journey with openness and curiosity— and with the ability to bestow limitless smiles and burbles and chuckles on all of Earth's adoring humans who would come to bask in the glow of our innocence!

Most of us eventually adjusted to the density of the Earth, often following that colicky stage when we were not sure how we ended up here, and why we had to stay. Eventually, we looked around with clear eyes and curious minds, and with one ear tuned to those Shining Ones who were still singing to us. As time went on, some continued to see those Shining Ones, to walk and talk with the spirit worlds even into adulthood. Some were called by voices only they could hear and went on to found evolutionary movements, societies, countries, and to irrevocably change the face of our world.

For most of us, however, our first and most dramatic of moments was the last of such a colossal magnitude in this lifetime. We were each that simple baby who ate, slept, cried, burbled, gurgled, and did all the things an ordinary baby does, on all the correct statistical timelines. We went on to be relatively obedient and loving little children, curious and rebellious teenagers, and, ultimately, responsible and hard-working adults. At our worst, we thought ourselves a tad boring, and perhaps not always useful as humans. At best, we had a few wildly amusing and creative moments.

Perhaps, we wondered, as we carried on about our adult lives: after all the miraculous drama of our birth, are we not supposed to continue having deep mystical journeys and apocalyptical rebirths? For are we not in an era of expansion, raising our vibration, communing with our soul groups, attaining ascension, on the cusp of a new golden age? Why did we not receive the call to lay down our lives, renounce ourselves to a higher calling, fire up the masses, to march the crusader's path?

Let's rewind a little. For those not at retirement as I am, please fast forward. There was playtime, then schooling, then jobs, relationships, marriages, births, deaths, kids, houses, cars, holidays, cooking, cleaning, buying, selling, blond hair, black hair, blue hair, skinny jeans, mom jeans (I wish I could say my skinny jeans have returned, but alas, no), spike heels and ruined metatarsals, dramatic statements that never entirely played out, minor details that became major wars (whatever was I thinking!). Some entertaining moments. Many very nice moments.

Undoubtedly, we contributed something of value to someone, somewhere along the way. I can see you all shaking your heads in agreement. Of course, I did, you say. We all did, did we not? Not such a bad life, really. I suppose that is the key then, to being able to say, "Not such a bad life."

A kale smoothie comes to mind. Yes, life is a kale smoothie. Six ingredients, medium-sized, goes down and stays down, neither goopy nor runny, moderately sweet on the tongue, mildly astringent aftertaste, a color somewhere between mud and grass. I admit I am not fond of kale smoothies unless the kale taste is smothered in sweet fruit and maple syrup, but there is something honest in its ordinariness, its down-to-earthiness.

So, most of the time we drink that kale smoothie because it is good for us. I mean, really, who walks around eating unadorned kale all day because they just cannot get enough of that grassy taste? So, my kale smoothie life seems a bit dull and boring, but like the kale, I tell myself the pure earthiness of it is very good for me, everyone around me and my descendants—healthier genes and such!

Many of us spend our lives in the same town where we are born. We have a simple job, a little house, several kids, two cars, one vacation per year, retire, sit on the porch, and eventually go to our final sleep. Simple human. How, you say, does our simple life make any difference at all? It seems a bit anti-climactic after all the drama of the arrival, the excitement of those Shining Ones bathing us in their love and encouragement with such joy and urgency!

Before the advent of fantasy movies, video games, a global internet, and reality TV, the world was a more straightforward place in many aspects. It may have been a bit easier to determine our place in the world. Societies evolved around closer-knit geographical and political units, and, for the majority of us, there were often fewer choices .

Today, our psyches are constantly bombarded with larger than life creations. We are led to believe that we are the next rock star, the voice of the century, a billionaire in the making, or a

Superhero. Everywhere you turn, media outlets are proclaiming it is easy, anyone can do it, just read this book, take this course, audition here.

Wait! Maybe we did miss our calling. Could we be a Superhero in disguise? Of course, some of us are born into this world to invoke global change, to uplift mass consciousness, to found movements, religions, nations, and empires, to reshape the very face of the earth itself. This handful of world-changing humans goes by any number of names: crusader, revolutionary, explorer, pioneer, avatar, god, hero, martyr, and so on.

All the powers of the Universe support them as they step onto their path to change the world. In the retelling and writing down of Earth's history, we highlight the world-changers taking center stage, again and again, their exploits often overlaid with a fuzzy dash of romance from the benefit of hindsight. That is what makes a great story.

Statistically, though, this is a small percentage of the billions of humans on the planet. By focusing on the few who rise up to steer a new course, we lose sight of those who were an integral part of our evolutionary process.

What happened after the world-changers had done their job, delivered their message, won the revolution, established the nation, changed the laws? This is the part that gets a few pages of bridging text in the history books until the next world-changer steps onto the stage. Something like, "The nation prospered, industry and manufacturing carried on apace, money was made, profits soared, import-export flourished, stock markets rebounded." Sounds a bit like "and they all lived happily ever after," doesn't it?

Someone had to carry the world forward. The basics of life on our planet had to keep functioning. The new philosophies brought forward by the world-changers had to be integrated by individuals, as well as by society. Someone had to do this, day after day, month after month, year after year—indeed, moment to moment. These were the countless legions of other humans who

22

passed through the ages of this world. In the history books, we can find them under the collective labels: ordinary, worker bees, plebeians, the average man on the street, the masses, John and Jane Doe, the proletariat, citizens, serfs, peasants, the 99%.

Who were they, who are they? Why do we not focus on them? I bet they were pretty interesting people in their own way. I am confident their contribution was as essential as those in the spotlight.

Ah, I have it! The majority of us are like Mr. Bailey, played by the endearing Jimmy Stewart, in the movie *It's a Wonderful Life*! All we need do is look at what would have happened if we had never been born.

Let's see…my spouses would have had other spouses, my parents would still have my brothers and maybe another one to fill in my spot, the corporation would have hired another person in my job. I did not save anyone from drowning or from otherwise annihilating themselves, at least that I can remember. I was an average student, not all that creative or innovative, so I created no new steam engines or flying machines or talking boxes. I didn't save anyone from bankruptcy, I foiled no global conglomerates or attempts to steal the town silver. I didn't have a chance to pull out my Superhero cape and miraculously save our way of life. Another family would have raised their cute little kids in my charming little yellow house, although it might not be the sunny yellow color that makes the neighbors smile over their morning cup o' java.

Let's be real, I tell myself. My life is just not that 'larger than life.' For most of us, life has little fanfare, few fireworks, no shape-shifting or physics bending, no story of horror or near-death or out-of-body experience. For most of us, life is placing one foot ahead of the other as best we can, so we can keep on 'keeping on.' Simply living, loving, smiling, frowning, wishing, grieving, hurting, laughing, crying, questioning, demanding, receiving, giving, and so on, unto the end. Simple humans leading simple lives.

When I was sketching out the outline for this book, I initially held kale smoothies to be bland, boring, and ordinary. Mr. Bailey was several notches above average, and Superheroes were extraordinary. We think we must categorize ourselves into either a Kale Smoothie, Mr. Bailey, or a Superhero. In fact, we do not ever. There is a niggling feeling within me of something that supersedes all that. That transcends the hierarchical structure in which we live that views everything as more significant than or lesser than.

This polarity concept applied to every little thing in our lives creates endless competition, ultimately breeding unconscious desperation. In truth, our world is morphing ever so gradually to a flat line structure where all are equal. How and where does this equality lie?

I returned to that moment of birth. The joy of the Shining Ones. The purity of the newly born

Soul. The fresh Light entering the world. The Light.

We are born from the Light. We are made of the Light. We are born with equal amounts of Light.

This is what equality really means. This is the true definition of Oneness—our indivisible and inseparable origin in the Light. We carry this Light inside us all the days of our Earth walk. We decide how brightly it will shine and how far it will radiate.

Although everyone is innately aware of this Light, over the years it can fade to a distant memory. Our light can dim. Things happen. Life happens. We encounter troubles. Challenging events cast shadows. We may feel lost and wounded. We might even experience Soul loss. The Light we celebrated at our birth becomes a distant memory, and, at best, we have fleeting remembered moments or a flash here and there. At worst, we feel entirely unplugged and lost in the black ooze.

Unlike Earthly light sources, however, our Light never extinguishes unless we choose to extinguish it and exit this Earth. It was with us before we entered this world and it will remain with us after we've left.

This Light is a far more critical attribute than any of our human characteristics. This Light is our power. In this power lies our equality. It is our Light that levels the playing field. Our inner Light adds a unique frequency to the world. No two of us project Light identically. Although equal in power, each carries a unique palette of colors, so to speak.

The truth is we are all world-changers. We all walk the path of the Lightkeeper. Each step on this sacred path trails in its wake a glittering rainbow that glows like the million stars in the inky dark sky at our birth.

I dreamed *I was hovering on the edge of a vast canyon of red rocks. Far below, a ribbon of water threaded the earth in serpentine swirls. The light was an eerie green glow, the clouds were low overhead. A force was urging me to jump off, and in the magical way of dreams, I found myself on the canyon floor, ambling upriver. It felt right as if I was headed for something familiar.*

Ahead in the distance was a muted splash of light. As I approached, it began to feel different—still familiar, but not friendly. I could feel the soft sand beneath my bare feet, again feel the warm wind blowing down through the walls. It all looked serene; nevertheless I hesitated, sensing that what I would see was not going to be to my liking.

An eagle soared down from the heights above,

looked me in the eye and beckoned. It flew, and I followed.

As I walked, I could feel the desert coming to life. It was as if the small plants and flowers were bending toward me, animals were coming out of their burrows in curiosity. I sensed Shining Ones were materializing through the canyon walls, Medicine Men and Women, elders of the ancient tribes who once inhabited that land, the spirits of my ancestors. They filed in silently behind me.

By the time I stood in front of that veil of light, I was backed by thousands of beings all feeding me courage and love and support. My feeling of dread was stronger than ever, but the compulsion to step through that veil was more than I could control.

The land on the other side was bleak and dry. As I looked around in puzzlement, an enormous creature ambled toward me from a distance. It was a dinosaur, old and tired and grey, very discouraged and disheartened. It led me to a strip of land that was wasted and dead and beckoned me to look closely at the scenes on either side. On the one side was a lush, beautiful landscape teeming with life, with forest, lakes, rivers, blue skies, all manner of colorful birds and small creatures. On the other was dry sand with dead things blowing about in the hot, suffocating wind.

I asked where we were and was told the "land-in-between," a neutral zone of no dimension, time, or space. The dinosaur impatiently beckoned me to look again on either side and understand. The land of the desert was where I dwelled. The land of lush life was waiting for me if I chose.

The dinosaur shooed me away. As I moved to step back through the veil into the canyon, it seared me with a look that held a weariness beyond caring. One word was branded on my mind. Endurance.

I embraced the dinosaur in gratitude, and that is when the magic happened. It literally melted into me. I shuddered from head to toe as it entered every cell of my body. As it flowed through me, I felt a shift, as if my body had previously been tilted and was now balanced and straight.

I walked back to the river and out of the crystal veil as that world dissolved into the air. Eagle was waiting to escort me back up the riverbed. It was here that another miracle happened.

As I walked, the thousands of Beings that had waited on the other side of the veil of light surrounded me with joy, touching me in blessing, as if I was a long-lost friend finally come home.

3

Life as a Kale Smoothie

Endurance.

The land of the desert represented living in an unconscious, unaware state. The lush area represented living in full awareness in my Soul and in the Light. The barren strip in between was the dead zone where no choice was taken either way. The dinosaur was grey, lifeless, and shadowed in this land-in-between ruled solely by the grim task of enduring moment to moment.

Endurance is a useful skill to cultivate. It is required in times of danger or stress or pushing to reach a goal. However, that is not the way we are meant to live every day. If we live every situation as if it is one big endurance test, there is no joy in the creations of our life.

We are not born into this world to merely survive and be a slave to other's values and creeds. We are not born to a life purpose that is all about lessons to be learned or obstacles to be overcome in a continuous pattern of servitude to some external force in the belief we are somehow bettering ourselves.

Which brings me back to that kale smoothie and the perceived need to decide whether we are a world-changer or a simple human. Let's imagine the smoothie ingredients are birth, childhood, schooling, careers, partners and dependents, elderhood. Mmm…a goopy mess. What is the glue that holds this successfully together, that keeps it from flying into disjunct globules and bitter flavors?

Today's world is so cluttered. We are like serial hoarders, burying our Self beneath layer upon layer of 'stuff' that we think the world demands of us, or that we feel we must demand of ourselves. Hidden in plain sight is another way to be that cuts through these complexities and powers up our humanity. This other way is the glue that binds the goopy mess into a smoothie that flows sweetly and gently to nourish body, mind, and Soul.

In truth, it does not matter whether we are called to lead a revolution or live a simple life. These are simply the roles on our to-do list of life. These are fluid and changeable. What matters is *how* we do what we do on that to-do list. This is the most essential element of our life. This is the glue that binds our smoothie. How we do what we do is what creates meaning in our lives.

We all want a life that has meaning. We think it is something to seek or create outside of ourselves. Such a focus on external events is like watching the hands of a clock move around its face. What we truly seek is meaning in our lives, in every moment. This is found in the internal working of our being. It is like the mechanism inside the clock that causes the hands to move around its face.

Live in the moment. Be in the moment. To experience meaning in our life does not entail cramming volumes of adventures into our bucket list, although that can be boatloads of fun! Instead, let's look for the fullness of meaning in the experience of each moment.

Our planet functions according to numerous natural and physics laws that create the impression of a linear order derived from mathematical units. In fact, all we are ever experiencing is a series of present moments. These string together in our memory. At the end of our physical time on Earth, we look back and call this our life. Do you remember what you did on day 2 of the 9th month at the 21st second of the 12th hour of the

4th year of your life? No, but I bet you do remember the first time you ate the juiciest of peaches left over from the summer harvest.

I was on a retreat long ago dipping my toe into the previously unknown waters of yoga and meditation. Six days of bliss! I remember trying to be perfectly dressed, always mindful to look blissful and serene like the more experienced yogis. No frown wrinkles or strange muscle twitches! I was trying to blend in, to fit in, not really knowing what that meant, so I thought if I looked the part, all would be fine. There was one woman who was particularly beautiful in her serenity—no frown wrinkles anywhere! I thought she was so terribly stately, elegant, lovely.

One morning I was out on the porch sipping my pre-dawn tea and heard a commotion around the corner. The lovely woman was raging in anger, voice raised and cursing in several languages. A few hours later, she was sitting blissfully in class.

I was shocked at first, but of course, it was an excellent lesson for me.

We are programmed from birth to believe that our existence operates on two separate levels. That the Soul and the human, which were one at birth, are rightfully dislocated over time as we fully integrate into the Earthly world. This is like a meditation retreat cycle. By the end of a retreat, we are in what we believe to be a permanent state of kindness and serenity. The return to the usual challenges of life gradually pricks that bubble. After a few months, we decide we really need to go back on retreat to reconnect to our serenity. Once again, we return to the world and poof, back to our irritations. I lived this cycle, and it puzzled me. Clearly, I was missing the point somewhere.

The point is harmony. A congruent life is a result of harmonizing our human self with our Soul. Once aligned, life becomes a continuous expansion of our potential to create in the material those things that embody our Soul's intent. Once harmonized, the sacred and secular merge to become one unified way of being.

We spend most of our energy trying to figure out what to do with our life. The words most often used are to figure out what we are supposed to do, as if there is a predetermined path decided upon at birth. This is a massive red herring. The 'to do' is a linear process of creating food and shelter and procreating to continue the species—acquisitions and mergers so to speak. The 'to be' is a Light-centered, non-linear state, an unfolding spiral of Soul manifestations. The 'to-do' is meaningless without the 'to-be.' We are engineered to do both and be both at the same time.

What elevates us above endurance into joy is our Light. We are spiritual beings whose purpose is to link to our Light, which is our lifeline to our Source. The expression of our being's Light is through our Soul. The operation of our being is our human body, maintained to be a vessel capable of manifesting the expressions of our Soul.

Our entire life is a sensory experience to uncover our essence and to express that essence. That is the experience and the sensation that lights us up at the end of the day. Everything we do as humans is experiential. We experience a thing through our senses to enable full comprehension of its meaning.

Watch a baby eating its food. All of its senses are engaged; in addition to taste, smell, touch, its body is relaxed and alert, its emotions are expressed, its Soul is calm, it is nourished. As we go about the tasks that our logical mind has set for our survival or pleasure, as an example, notice how our Soul is telling us to randomly smile at someone. Notice how it shows us the deep pain beneath a colleague's habitual expression of anger. Shining our Light could pierce the hurt so that person might begin to express and heal.

The Light shining through our Soul is so bright that it can shift the energies around us. As

I enter my seventh decade on this planet, I am coming to understand the immense power that flows from our pure and simple souls, leading Light-filled lives. These carry our world forward one step at a time, one life experience at a time. It is about being. Being in the present, on time, there, alive, awake, aware, living from your Light at all times. I have seen this power leave a wake of transformation billowing out behind that will impact generations to come.

The Light-filled life carries an energy so powerful in its simplicity that it can tap the forces of the Universe and bring about its own quiet revolution, one Soul, then another and another. We cease to worry so much about what we are doing because all that we do is so filled with Light that it can never cause any harm. This requires surrendering our logical mind and allowing our intuitive heart to be in the dominant position.

If Light is genuinely such a powerful force, the next question might be: "what is it?" This force is only as valuable as it is actionable in our daily lives. To take us to the heart of our existence, this Light must be something readily available to us, that we can access easily, work with, understand. There must be a simplicity to it that perhaps we have missed, living as we do in such a complex world.

Where is this Light? To be such a powerful force, it must reside in the most prominent place within each of us.

I dreamed *I was floating weightlessly in a field of black oily goo. It expanded and reformed like viscous lava as I moved. It had no form; it held no structure. It was like trying to move within the sticky web of a giant spider.*

It was everywhere pressing on me, suffocating me. My lungs were breathing it in. My body was filled with it. I cried out, but no sound came forth. I looked, but no Light penetrated to comfort me.

In utter helplessness, I withdrew into myself, sending feeble tendrils of thought outward, hoping something, anything, was out beyond this. I felt myself letting go, shutting down.

Suddenly, the dark ooze shifted like curtains parting, and a shaft of light appeared. It arrowed its way to me as I instinctively turned towards it. As it came closer, it took the shape of a star. There was a center point holding the brilliance of a powerful sun. Rays of light shot out in all directions. It pulsed, it glittered, it shone. It was beautiful. It was alive.

It was dangerous! It was not just any star; it was our own Sun star coming straight for me. I thought it would surely incinerate me, and this was my ending.

Miraculously it slowed its approach. It landed gently on my heart and then penetrated deeply until I felt it in all parts of my body. It expanded until I was filled with the most brilliant Light. I was the Sunstar! The Sunstar was me! There was no beginning and no end. We were one.

The black oily ooze retreated, burned away by the power of this Light. In an instant, I was back on Earth with this Sunstar intact and radiating around me. A soft, melodious voice whispered, "As above, so below."

4

Our Personal Sun

Our Sun. Our galaxy Sun. Our personal Sun. It comes from without and resides within. It took some pondering for me to go beyond the apparent absurdity of this in material terms to what lay in the deeper mystical levels. As I stood in the center of the dream-vision notes that prompted this writing, rotating through some sort of vortex, I had been shown there was a central point around which all that we are turns.

Each time I meditated on this, similar messages came through. Reverse your perspective...

turn 180 degrees...look from the outside in and not the inside out...look from the Soul in at the human, not from the human out at the Soul. "As below, so above. As above, so below. As without, so within. As within, so without." Curiously, "it is not what you think" came through over and over.

We naturally look at everything as if we are the beginning of the center point of the Universe. Imagine that we could transport ourselves outside the Universe and look in. Astronauts have a brief taste of this perspective. On one occasion, I, too, had an experience of this. During one deep meditation, my consciousness seemed transported way out beyond our galaxy, and I was looking down at it. It was not a part of me. It felt foreign. It appeared as a bubble created by a master glassblower. Our galaxy and our Earth were inside the glass. I was outside blowing the bubble.

I was a Soul in its original form. Outside looking in. Above, searching below. From this altered perspective, I began to wonder what was truly happening here for us humans. Why were Souls incarnating here, over and over again in most cases? And what did this have to do with Light and Suns?

The Sun is the central star of our solar system. It generates life, light, heat, sustenance, growth. It powers our cycles, our night and day, sleep and awake, climate, seasons. It fosters cycles of life and death, creation, and destruction. The Sun fills us with feelings of relaxation, calm, and peace when we turn our faces to it. The beautiful force of this star can cause our mind to stall its chatter and go momentarily blank as if being hit with some otherworldly sensation.

The Sun powers the rotation of the planets, and stars through a gravitational pull. Lighter objects orbit heavier objects. The Sun is the most massive object in our system. It binds all in a never-ending orbit around its brilliant, life-giving self.

If "as above, so below, as below, so above" is true, then our human physical form must mirror our planetary system. There must be a central element within our bodies around which the rest of it rotates. As the Sun holds all planets together, so our inner sun binds us together and keeps us magnetized, electrified, and formed within our energy blueprint.

Our own personal version of the Sun feeds all the mysterious systems that keep us alive and thriving here in the below, as a mirror of the Sun in the galaxy above. The more I contemplated this, the more I could see it everywhere, from the microscopic to the macroscopic. We are a micro version of our Universe. From powering the individual cells in our tissues to powering the frequencies of our external relationships to powering group consciousness.

I had images of seeing every element of life on Earth and in the galaxies. All was spinning in a seemingly random fashion, yet in total coherence— as above, as below, so below, so above, no beginning, no end. Contracting and expanding in tune with the force of creation, powered by the Light of this Sun. As the Sun projects power in our solar system, so too does our inner sun provide such potential for us.

What makes the world go 'round? We commonly answer this phrase with money or love or the trendy word of the day. In truth, it is us, we humans, that makes the world go 'round. The world we create revolves around and evolves from, the quality and intensity of the Light of the central sun within us. All of our energy frequencies radiate from this point. It is powerful beyond our comprehension. Our capacity to hold, to keep and to focus the Light through our inner sun is what makes the world prosper or stagnate, be healthy or diseased, be filled with love or filled with fear.

In my dream-vision, the Sun radiated a brilliant Light within me, pushing away the darkness. The word Light is used over and over by many and has been since the beginning of language. Light makes us feel warmth, hope, vitality, relief, relaxation, health, comfort, peace, serenity. The more we use a word, the more it becomes lodged at the forefront of our mind. We pull it out often and use it to signify something that we assume all will understand the same way. This can sometimes result in the loss of a word's actual definition.

Let's return to the dream of the newborn at the beginning. The Light of the baby's inner sun is as bright as can be at this time of life, unspoiled by conditioning and external experiences. Think for a moment about how we connect with a baby. Babies have no language, other than the unique messages in their cries. A newborn sees only light waves, unable to focus and categorize these into recognizable objects.

Yet, despite this seeming handicap, when we look into its eyes, we perceive a connection, a transmission to us and from us to them. This connection is like two ends of an electrical current joining their frequencies. We understand what this is, a sense that goes far beyond the language of our conscious mind to the deepest core of our being. The connection happens through our Light.

This Light is the beam coming from our Source. Our Source-Creator that is the cosmic birther—the Unmanifest, the Divine Intelligence, the Eternal One, the All in All. The Unnamable that we try so very hard to name. The Light is that bit of the Source's essence that It shares with each of Its creations, the Divine Spark, so to speak.

The definition of essence is that which is the inner nature or pure substance of a thing. The full reality of Source cannot be known to us in our human form, as we are too frail by comparison. Our further inadequacy is such that we can only define things within the limits of our Earthly understandings. Yet, we have each been given life through this tiny filament of indefinable essence.

"There are beautiful and wild forces within us." Attributed to St Francis of Assisi, these frail words attempt to describe the primal, visceral nature of this Light we carry. In all creation stories, Light is the first element called into being.

Creative energy is wild and unordered, needing to be claimed and focused.

It is the Light that brings the order, that tames the wildness and the unsettled waters. Before there were creatures in this creation, there was the Light that formed them. It shines through our inner sun as fiery as the galaxy Sun itself. Its purity does not take away from its primal, unconstrained, and wondrous nature.

Creation is an act of Source to create for the sheer delight of creating. The new creation is looked upon, experienced, and cherished. It is like the painter and the painting. The painting is us, and the painter is the Source. We cannot exist without Source, yet it can exist without us. It imbues us with a tiny spark of its creative essence. It looks on us with delight and wonderment for having created us, just as we would look at a painting that we created with joy and wonder for having done so.

Source loves Its creations so much that It creates a link through our Soul. As our Soul travels out on its own, the link is always intact, like a child leaving home. Source cannot force or direct us, yet it remains intimately close should we choose to activate the link and receive the fullness of its Light.

The way of the Lightkeeper is our relationship with our Creator. As we strengthen that connection through Its Light, we return to our senses. When did that phrase come to mean being in our logical mind? It means a return to our visceral senses. First, we sense, then we know, then we think to define and describe. Life is about the experience of this Light in all forms and expressions as felt through our senses. Here we know all we need to know.

This Light is like a wireless frequency. We are a conduit/generator keeping the frequency of Light always in motion, moving between its Source and our inner sun, then out from us to connect with other beings. We then attract Light to us that feeds back to Source. Source responds by sending us more Light, which generates the cycle all over again. The originating point within our personal sun radiates Light around us and out through all dimensions. When the Light flows freely, it becomes a larger and larger field rippling around us like a star.

Like a bodybuilder we must do things to strengthen that muscle of our personal sun, so to speak. To keep it alive and flexible and the Light flowing freely within us, spinning continuously to emanate its frequencies. To be received and returned in an endless loop. It grows in power as the circuit is exercised. It becomes more significant the more we tend it.

Light creates Light. We are fashioned to be centered in this Light always. It is not to be something we are born with and grow out of as we mature. We need to feel ourselves smack dab in the center of this Light. We need to be spinning in the swirling vortex of kaleidoscopic frequencies to realize that this Light we talk about is a real, tangible, and vibrant essence. It is the tiny spark of the delight of our Source with Its creation. It is our life.

When our connection to this Light is active, fascinating things happen to us. Physically we stand straight with chest high and balanced torso. Emotionally we feel joy. Mentally we are measured and calm and hold an unshakeable belief in something beyond our bubble of Earth. Ethereally, there are waves of bright energy bands circulating evenly outwards from us. Spiritually these bands are intelligent enough to be recognized by our Source, and communication through our Soul becomes direct and effective.

"I just want to find my home, to have that place where I feel I belong and can feel secure. Where I am loved simply for who and what I am!" How often we hear these words from our own lips as well as many others'. We think of home as a place or thing or person. Or we believe we must leave our body and this Earth to go home to some mythical dimension.

In truth, we are meant to find the way home while we are living. We perceive it in the Light that flows through our Soul. This Light is all we are and all we require. It arrived here without our physical body, and it will leave here without our physical body.

"Send out your Light, let it bring me to your dwelling." In the Celtic tradition, Light is liberated, or let loose, from the heart of creation, the heart of the Source-Creator. Like the prodigal son, we must eventually have our fill of this Earth's experiences of separation.

"Send out your Light" is a cry from our heart exhorting our Source to send its Light to us so that we may find our way back home. Home to the unity with Source, from whence we came.

I dreamed *I was lying on a slab of rock. Black volcanic obsidian. Forged from the primordial ooze in the time before memory. It was cold and smooth and radiated mesmerizing waves that drew my body into it like sinking through fluffy white clouds.*

There was fire. A vivid dance of oranges, yellows, and reds encircled me. It leaped and curled, yet there was no heat, and I was not afraid. I stretched out a hand to touch it, and the flames tickled my skin. I waited. For something. My mind went blank, and I surrendered to sensation.

Suddenly, there was a stirring of the flames behind my head. I sensed something there. A being? Many beings? The Shining Ones? Still, I was not afraid, yet I had no desire to turn and look. Calmly, I waited.

Deep within I knew something was about to take place.

It happened. A geometric shape was poured in through my head down through my body where it settled softly in my core. It appeared to my inner vision as an upside-down pyramid. Point facing down.

Immediately it was followed by another shape. This one was a point-side-up pyramid. In an instant, the two fused within me to a diamond shape. I could still make out the faint line where the bases of the pyramids met. Strange.

I felt nothing traumatic or uncomfortable, only a gentle expansion within. It was as if I had previously been shrink-wrapped and was now stretched out to a more comfortable and flexible size and shape.

At this point, my curiosity overcame me, and I turned my inner vision to investigate. I had a vague sense of shimmery veils of light which winked out immediately, and I woke up.

5

The Diamond Within

After this dream-vision, I noticed that I felt very different. My body was more relaxed and fluid as if the boundaries of my outer skin had thinned from six inches to a quarter inch. As if my inner self was now one with the external world and my physical body was a thin intrusion between. My mind felt open-ended, like a filing room that previously had one cabinet within and now had infinite rows of cabinets. My perspective was broad, and I felt tethered to something greater than myself.

I did not physically look any different. My organs were still ticking along. The health boo-boos I was working through were still there—sigh! Yet I experienced all this differently. It felt as if several additional senses had been added to the familiar ones. These were new sensations that I had to explore more. Of course, the geometric shape was also intriguing to me!

Shortly after this dream-vision, I woke up one morning lying on my back. At first opening, my eyes focused on a point off the foot of my bed. There I saw a diamond-shaped light about four feet tall. It was hanging, suspended in space and shimmering faintly! My room was dark, with blackout blinds, so no accidental sun rays were filtering through the window. It was a distinct diamond, just hanging out, waiting for me to see it. As soon as I realized what I was seeing and focused consciously on it, it faded away.

The symbolism of a diamond is profound.

Arguably it is one of the most aesthetically beautiful substances on Earth. It is also the most durable. Its name is from the Greek word adamas, meaning unconquerable. With these valuable properties, its applications range from medicine to timekeeping, to industrial manufacturing, technology, and more. A pure diamond is the most transparent and natural material known. It reflects visible light, ultra-violet and infrared light, and all the frequencies in between. Diamonds are also an insulator or a conductor.

For thousands of years, the diamond shape has been a symbol of a sacred union. It is no coincidence that the slogan, "a diamond is forever," symbolizes undying romantic love. The classic diamond shape has been used to express ascension, spiritual power, the seer, healer, lightworker, psychic, sage, and more.

In the dream-vision, the double-diamond shape formed on my physical body connecting my throat, right shoulder, solar plexus, left shoulder, and back to my throat. Visualize this shape in a three-dimensional form that flows through the body from front to back and top to bottom like the kind of sparkling, spinning top we played with as a child.

This visualization triggered a recall of my very first dream-vision, many years earlier. That event happened through the beat of a drum in the masterful hands of a yogi-shaman. I suddenly remembered that the rhythm, tempo, and intensity of the sound waves had struck me in the diamond! Not just the heart or solar plexus, but in the entire area that I was now seeing as a diamond.

I recalled I had felt my heartbeat synchronize to the drumbeat, which is not so unusual. But that my solar plexus had also been pulsing, my thymus was pulsing, and my throat was vibrating. All these physical parts had awakened and were pulsing with the beat! When they came together in one synchronized sensation, I had been transported out of my body and into a dream-vision.

If we were to strip away our physical structure—our bodies, organs, muscle and bones—and strip away the illusion of the dense, solid matter that makes up our Earth—the rocks, trees, plants, houses, furniture—there remains our primal essence. This vibrating essence carries a unique signature, one belonging solely to me, and another to you, and so on for every creature. It powers how and what we bring forth in our lives physically and emotionally, as well as how we view our lives mentally and spiritually.

Imagine it to be a dot of Light in the center of your body. Your heart beats and the dot of Light pulses in rhythm. Your mind, your breath, and your body come alive and pulse to the rhythm of this Light. Our personal Light signature is generated here from the Source frequencies that flow into it. This dot of Light is the vibrational center of our being, around which all that we are revolves like a mini-galaxy.

This dot is our inner sun, the physical and energetic spot at the core of our being where our heart rests. Here in this space, the essence of Source, Its spark of Light, Its delight flows into us. Here in this central sun of our heart, we find our Light which powers our life after leaving the womb. It is the translator and connector to our Source.

Here we accept that essence and process it into the attributes that serve our human existence. Close your eyes and turn off all your external senses. See yourself without a mirror. We have spent our lives looking at our reflections in a mirror. In it, we see only the outline of our outer skin. This exterior is not us. Try to imagine you had never seen your outer surface in a mirror. All you would know is a sense of yourself that flows from your inner sensations.

Our physical structure cannot hold the full power of Source's frequency, due to the density of matter. However, our heart is made of a substance that transcends this density. It is structured to attract, magnify, and project many times more than our other energy centers. The more it attracts, the more it will expand, and the more it becomes able to contain. It has an infinite capacity to channel the essence of Source.

Hundreds of years ago, the heart was referred to as the principal place, the center of a circle, the middle of the necessary body. Thousands of years ago it was referred to as the center of metaphysical interpretations and the primary spiritual member of the body. I am not the first to call it the king or sun of the body to underscore its significance.

The heart has been called the brain of the new age to come. It is the first functional organ to develop in the womb and starts to beat around day 22. The brain begins to function around a week after the heart. There is some research today that says the heart sends more signals to the brain than the other way around. The heart influences the brain, just as the brain affects the heart.

The heart is the first organ to grow because it is the portal through which the essence of our Creator-Source enters to make us a living physical embodiment of our Soul. Through our heart, the beam of Source is received— and also returned. Through this Light within us, we are also feeding Source. It takes delight in Its creation; therefore, It wants to feel what Its creation feels. Think of the pleasure we take in experiencing what our children experience. We see a sandcastle or a sunset with a renewed sense of awe and delight through their eyes.

Similarly, all that our Soul experiences is looped back to be fully experienced by Source. The entire process of life is made simple when we understand the Light we hold. What it is, why we have it, and what we are to do with it is the real reason we are here. The answers to all such questions are found in dialogue with our Soul—not in conversation with our mind. Once this Soul dialogue begins, more and more Light floods in through our heart sun.

When the heart space is fully open, the Light overflows around and through the diamond of our core. The diamond area acts as an amplifier and projector; we are filled with the power of this Light and become this Light. Within our physical bodies, this Light powers our cells, frees us from dis-ease, powers our fluidity, flexibility, our lightness, strength, and endurance. Within our minds, it fuels our positive thought, our clarity, and decisiveness. Within our emotions, it colors an infinite rainbow of empathy, compassion, affection. It burns away fear, anger, heaviness, density, negativity, judgment.

Ask yourself, "How is my Light doing?" Is it small or large, in the center of the diamond, even overflowing around the diamond? Does it touch the points of the diamond? Does it encompass our will, our voice, our load-bearing capacity?

The solar plexus is the seat of our personal will. In simple terms, our will is our ability to direct ourselves beyond our primitive animal survival reflexes. The solar plexus is the center from which we make choices. We can choose to direct ourselves towards fulfilling only basic survival strategies. We can choose to lead our will to an expanded consciousness. When we decide to go beyond survival instincts, we are confronted with all the questions that our society places on the spectrum of good to bad, right to wrong, positive to negative. As conscious choice requires more complex thought patterns than primitive instinct, we often make it more complicated than it needs to be.

The throat holds our capacity to voice our Soul. Is it open or closed, choked, squeaky, or growly? Are the words that emanate from here those of someone else, or our creations? Are they from our expanded consciousness or our survival instincts? Are we overusing or underusing this voice of ours? Are we saying too much when a kind smile would suffice, electing to withhold when another needs reassurance or praise? Are we by-passing our Soul's authenticity and speaking facile nonsense?

The shoulders represent our capacity to carry our life. To shoulder or shed, to duck, to collapse, to straighten, to project. The front and back of the shoulders have slightly different jobs. Opening the front releases pressure on the heart. It lifts the rib cage so the solar plexus (our will) can energetically merge with our heart. It opens the throat for calmness of breathing and speaking from the heart. If we had physical wings, they would be on our back, tucked by the shoulder blades. This rear area represents our capacity to fly, to take off, to move. These imaginary wings can become pinched or stretched, strong or weak, large or tiny. We most often think of shoulders as the area related to our burdens. To shoulder our burdens is an age-old phrase. Circumstances are only burdens if we label them such. Labels create illusions. Circumstances are simply circumstances. Strength around our shoulders keeps us upright and flying true, beyond such illusions.

The Light spirals out from our heart through our solar plexus (bottom point of the diamond) such that our personal will is firmed up and clear. It envelopes the throat (the top of the diamond) such that we think and speak from the attributes of this Light, our will merged with an expanded intention. It extends to the side points of the diamond near the shoulders such that the power that we are and the will that we hold enables us to shoulder with ease all that comes our way. We can move fluidly in all directions. To fly above all, if required. The more Light we funnel in, by opening wide our heart sun, the more we can hold.

Building strength and stability through our diamond core enables not only ourselves but all we come in contact with to be in that strength. It allows us to shift our environment to one of Light. It keeps us from falling into another's negativity. It gives us the will, the heart, and the voice to send Light into the world.

We have been gifted with this part of us that beats as a homing beacon from within our mother's womb to let our Creator know where we are.

The brighter the beam, the stronger the connection, not only with our Source but with each other as sisters and brothers in the unified family of Source's creations.

I dreamed I was standing at the bottom of an immense, towering cliff. I looked up along its face and saw it was impossible to climb. I felt trapped at its base. Very tiny, insignificant, uncertain. Searching intently, I glimpsed a faint light far up in the shadows.

Suddenly a beautiful lady appeared at the top edge. She tilted her head over the side and saw me cowering far below. Her face lit up as if she knew me well. She beckoned excitedly to me, and reached down, far down, clasped my hand and pulled me up!

The light I had glimpsed from below was a solid stone lighthouse perched high upon a rock facing out to sea. The lady was more beautiful than I could ever imagine, shimmering vibrantly in a white-gold dress and a blue cloak.

It was wild and chaotic on the bluff in the untamed elements, yet I felt no fear. We laughed as the wind whipped and lashed around us. The surf was crashing below, the tall grasses were bending to the ground, high clouds were racing across the sky. We reveled in the wildness.

Into the wind, she flung her hands, and sparks flew from her fingertips. Where they landed, all was Light. She took my hands, showed me how to do this, and together we sent Light of all colors to the ends of the earth.

All living things reached out eagerly to catch these Lights, that were like stars floating to earth. Each found a different colored star, and some caught many. All were instantly transformed.

The lady took my hands and looked deeply into my eyes. "All colors, all frequencies, all reside in all."

6

Our Prism Heart

Sometimes these dream-visions truly perplex me, yet they are so compelling, I cannot help but look for the meaning. I love puzzles and connecting the dots, as my spirit guides well know, so I received two other strange occurrences to nudge me toward understanding.

I have a square plate of shungite rock on which my cell phone rests. One morning after a meditation session, I entered my kitchen to check my phone and noticed some water had spilled along the counter around and under the shungite.

I absently picked up the stone to dry it and froze in place. The water had created a pattern on the underside of the plate.

It was the outline of a diamond, with a series of water dots in a perfect circle around the outside of the diamond and a dot of water in the center. Off to the left side, there was a tiny version of the same design made by more water droplets. I was stunned. My imagination was not making this up! I dutifully drew the images in my journal, in case my mind would later convince me it was fiction.

Sometime later I was binge-watching a Netflix series on astrophysics. I love astrophysics but had never before been so obsessively fixated, so I began to consciously pay attention for a potential message. Sure enough, three episodes later, the host introduced a segment that had nothing to do with astrophysics. He had decided to indulge a personal love of his and do a segment on prisms! Aha! There it was! Time for me to connect the dots—stars, colors, frequencies, diamonds...prisms!

A prism is one of the most elegant structures in our world, an object of beauty that transforms one thing into its smaller and more beautiful components. It is an element that can reflect, disperse, or split light into its parts. Shine a beam of light through a prism. It goes in looking like a single beam and comes out split into multiple rays of colors like a rainbow. Our physical eye most clearly distinguishes seven, though there are, in fact, an infinite number of color ray combinations exiting the prism, most not distinguishable to the naked eye.

Our hearts are the most elegant structure of our body, both in its physical and energy functions. Imagine our heart—our inner sun— as a prism with the capacity to receive a single beam of Light, split it into the qualities that make up that Light, and disperse these Rays all around us. This is how it works with the Source essence. It enters as one beam into our heart and our heart-prism projects to the world its infinite qualities and blends. I truly mean infinite. Our hearts have an unlimited capacity to capture, to hold, and to project.

The spark of our Source's essence is tiny by Its standard, but mighty by human standards. It is neither a special gift nor a blessing, it is the essential component of life. More than just sparking us to life, like the spark of a combustion engine, it is also our fuel supply. It is a fuel that we are intended to actively use, and it is the prism-like nature of our inner sun, our heart center, that breaks this frequency into humanly useable components.

Whatever this essence was, way back when the first creative event was set in motion by Source, I think it is safe to assume there was a great delight in the creating and in observing the new creation unfold. The spark flowing from the Source to us carries this delight to us. We genuinely possess no words to describe this otherworldly essence of happiness, yet we try. The word we typically agree upon is love.

Ah, love! I bet you wondered when I was coming around to that word. For as long as we can remember, we have used this word to describe the powerful essence of our Creator Source—phrases such as "the power of love derives from our Source," "the Source love lives in all of us," "God is love," and so on. I was born in the final years of the baby-boomer generation when our world was turned upside down with that glorious flower-power movement of 'make love, not war.'

Since that time, we have come to use that word love very loosely. Phrases such as "love you," "love that man," "great person, love her" trip off our tongue regularly. What we really mean to say is "accept her," "respect that man," "great person, I am in wonder of her ability to ...." These are the real words behind the glib use of the word love. Perhaps in some cases, we are also being untruthful as we do not accept, respect, or honor that person we have just said "love you" to.

Search a dictionary for the definition of the word love, and you get a soup-to-nuts list: an intense feeling of deep affection, a great interest, and pleasure in something, attraction based on sexual desire, admiration, benevolence or shared interests, emotional attachment. There are no less than 45 synonyms that range from the psychological to the conceptual (such as philanthropic), to the bizarre (such as intrigue)! The most-used word to define love is affection, which is a word most associated with the emotive aspect of being human.

In ancient times, love was defined by the Greeks based on what group it was bestowed upon— romantic, brotherly, charitable, children, divine, community. Recent history has added self-love to this list. Most cultures have similar designations and categories under different labels. These designations are more like the applications of love, rather than its essence. This is an understanding of love through the lens of the intellect. A very structured, logic-oriented view, which creates separation and a sense of distance from the thing to which we are applying the word.

Current voices narrow this to a more biological view: companionate, which is affection without physical arousal, and passionate, which is intense longing often accompanied by physical arousal; or an instinctive drive like hunger and thirst. Many eastern philosophies believe the nature of love is a mystical experience.

Language is a challenge. We live in a world full of words. We seem compelled to express with words everything we feel and sense. Words have become play toys. We mix them up in quirky ways, not always faithful to the definitions, but because they sound cool. We worship words as delivering the ultimate truths to us. We paste them on T-shirts, handbags, fridges, computers, calendars. The 6-word tag-line, the 30-second elevator pitch, the 240-character tweet.

Phrases initially designed to stop us in our tracks and bring on that aha moment of wonder and awe are now so commonplace that we notice very little wonder and awe anymore. And yes, the irony of me writing a book full of words is not lost on me! How often do we stop and ponder what the words truly mean and if we are using them in their proper context?

Love is one of those overused words. It has become so commonplace as to have lost its original sacred truth. And yet in our misuse of it, there is, of course, some truth! While intellectual or clinical definitions serve a function, they do not describe the essence that underlies and provides the foundation for the love we apply to a sibling, child, deity, partner, community, self. In defining love as we currently do, we have leaped over the essence of it to the applications of it and forgotten the most important part—its qualities.

Essence defines what something is made of as its base element. Source essence is complicated to describe in words. In fact, it not only does not adhere to any logical principles, but it also defies logic in many cases because it is a multi-dimensional frequency originating outside the realm of our three-dimensional world. Our prism heart helps us out with this by breaking this essence into useable human elements, the multiple qualities seen in my dream-vision as Rays. These Rays are what we apply to the infinite situations we experience in our life. These qualities dispersed through the prism of our hearts as Rays, we collectively refer to as love.

In my dream-vision, I was observing the qualities as stars with Rays of colors shooting out from their centers. The message was that all creatures are to receive all these Rays from all of us at all times. It matters not whether it be God or family or community. We are not meant to differentiate how we apply these Rays to any living creature. The Rays are the infinite number of ways we are to spin the Light through the prism of our hearts continuously in a field of energy that impacts everyone and everything. This also enters the web of energy that manifests our collective memory and global consciousness.

While it is clearly impossible to talk about all the infinitely variable qualities of these Rays, there were seven that were given to me in meditation as foundational to the essence we call love. These are wonder, respect, honesty, benevolence, purity, integrity, and impeccability.

Wonder is defined as surprise mingled with admiration, an extraordinary act or achievement, awe, and a feeling of reverential respect. Respect is deep admiration elicited by certain qualities, a regard for the opinions, wishes, and rights of others. Benevolent means well-meaning and kind.

Purity is freedom from contamination or extraneous elements. Impeccable is faultless and irreproachable in all things. Integrity means being whole and undivided. Honesty is defined as free of deceit and untruth.

I set myself a test to attempt to understand

these definitions in the context of the standard definitions of love. To begin, I spent much time focusing on the sensations these Rays created in my heart and diamond core. Then I practiced applying these in all my relationships. I can say that this exercise highlighted how often I was not in resonance with these Rays, even though I thought that I was!

As an example, let's look at family love. We are exhorted to automatically love our family because one classical definition of love is family. When we say we love them, do we know what we mean? Do we hold them in respect, benevolence, wonder? Do we always deal with them in integrity, impeccability, honesty? It is so easy to use the words, "I love my sister." Try substituting "I respect her, I honor her, I view her with wonder, with generosity."

Note what sensations show up in our body, as we focus in this way. We cannot say we truly love unless we hold wonder, respect, benevolence, purity, impeccability, integrity, and honesty within our heart, and project these to the subject of our love.

Any of these seven Rays can be subdivided again and again, like fractals, as they apply to unique personal situations. As an example, wonder contains elements such as reverence, respect includes elements such as acceptance and honor, benevolence includes factors such as generosity and mercy, purity contains innocence and hope, and so on.

The fractal principle became very clear when I began to focus on these in my daily life. No two situations are ever the same. There are infinite combinations of these seven Rays that we unconsciously blend. Some nuances shift like lightning. This shifting can entangle us along pathways of thought, word, and deed that we never intended.

I found it helpful to continually remind myself of the seven Rays through that little voice in the back of my mind. My mantra went something like, "Is this impeccable, is my integrity present, am I honest, was that respectful, did I find the wonder in this, did I hold to the purity of intent, was I kind?" "Back to basics. Cut the chatter. Park the nuance." It felt as if I was reverting to childhood, learning to think, speak, and act all over again. Over time, I found the Rays became so uppermost in my awareness that I had no more need to chant my inner mantras.

You may wonder why I did not include empathy, sympathy, and compassion in my list. These are perhaps most associated with love in our culture. They are not included because they are outcomes flowing from the Rays. The Rays are the cause, these are the effect, so to speak. When we live in the Rays of wonder, respect, benevolence, purity, integrity, impeccability, honesty, we will automatically and instinctively feel empathy, emanate sympathy, act with compassion, and grant mercy.

We give up nothing when we live in our Light. In fact, we add much. Think of this as musical harmonics. Each quality of the heart is like a separate tone conveying multiple overtones or frequencies. When we layer tone upon tone, we have the full chord. This fullness of harmony creates an infinite spectrum of frequencies. Such is the essence of Light we call Love.

There is a shift in our Soul-human field like an earthquake when we live in these Light Rays. We notice instantly where we are not genuinely emanating Light. We see clearly that the intellectual labeling of love as of a brother, child, friend, group creates separation into "us and them." When we focus on the Rays, we can no longer remain separate from others. We sense the oneness of all as it continually renews in us through the essence of Source.

*I **dreamed*** *I was in a place of silence. Actually, not a quiet, rather an intense stillness. There was no movement of air or sound or light. It was like a void, yet it was alive. There was an indefinable electric pulse in the space.*

My senses somehow attuned to this frequency, and I began to see. I was not alone. There were many others, each with different energy signatures that shimmered and blended into what appeared to be a group of beings. Not human, yet somewhat human-like. Shining Ones!

I attempted to count, and there seemed to be 12, but the concept of counting kept winking out as if to say the number was really of no consequence. It felt like a council of some sort. We were hovering around a large oval table, communicating through thought, discussing something of grave import. There was an urgent yet peaceful tone.

I heard a voice saying, "They will be given a choice."

That is when I noticed that we were all examining and passing around numerous starry objects. They were not stars: they just appeared that way to my inner vision. They were pulsing with a luminescence I had never before perceived. Each was of a brilliant color-ray combination.

I realized that what I was seeing was the purest of frequencies. Their movements emitted bursts of rays in star-like formations.

As soon as my mind latched onto this and began to 'think,' I woke up. Not with a start, but very peacefully, with full remembrance of the voice, the Shining Ones, the frequencies.

7

Choosing Light

Our most tantalizing gift is the ability to make a choice. Many attempt to convince us that choice is a complicated construct. So much emotion becomes attached to the 'either-or.' Whole forests are decimated to make lists of 'what if's.' We may not believe we can choose every element of our lives, but we can. We are not locked into a specific pattern of behavior or thought whatever the state of our external circumstances. Believing we have no choice is also a choice—a decision not to believe.

The either-or, what if thought process is a function of the polarity-duality properties of our three-dimensional world. Where we focus, there will we be. If we focus on cause and effect, we will create cause and effect. If we focus on manifesting matter, we will remain locked in matter. If we focus on the rhythm of the ripples of all that, we will perpetuate the ripples. If we focus on something being relative to something else, we will maintain separation from that other thing. If we function through reciprocal expectation, we create an infinite see-saw effect.

No matter how pure we believe our intention, if it is not of the Rays, we will automatically activate the laws of our dimension that create separation —the laws of polarity-duality.

We are polarized as long as we focus on duality, for as long as we believe that we are locked in an eternal see-saw that says for every action, there is an equal and opposite reaction. This principle means that for every act of horrendous darkness perpetrated somewhere around the globe, there will be a balanced reaction for the Light somewhere else in the world. In this way, balance is maintained.

A balance must always be maintained within this dimension, or this dimension will cease to exist. Therefore, as we pour good works into the world—with the intent of doing a good deed rather than sharing love—these will create an equal and opposite reaction somewhere else. When we ask for peace in one place, there will be a war somewhere else. It appears as an either-or choice, like the Panama Canal splitting the Americas, and we are programmed to jump back and forth between actions of Light and dark. The long years of human history have seen an endless repetition of this principle.

The summer of 2018 was one for the record. My husband and I were roaming and ended up close to the massive wildfires burning out of control along the west coast of North America. We had been driving through a haze of smoke for three entire Canadian provinces when we hit a situation neither of us had ever experienced. We were in northern Alberta on a major highway at two in the afternoon. Within the space of ten short minutes, we went from hazy yellow visibility to pitch black, and my cell lost connectivity.

The sun was completely blocked by the massive smoke cloud that roamed all over North America for weeks. For the next 30 minutes, we crawled slowly along with the other traffic. At one point we literally could not see the front hood of our truck. Our headlights could not penetrate the darkness! We could not see the rear lights of the transport in front of us. We could not even see the camper we were towing behind us!

For this short space in time, our reality narrowed to the two of us in a truck floating in a black void. It got me thinking about how it must have been hundreds of years ago when people had no way of finding out what was happening during such an event. They might have thought the world was ending.

The point is that our perception is so often

limited to what we can see. What we see is dependent on Light. I was looking everywhere for clues about what was going on outside my truck, but I could not see anything with my eyes. So my reality shrank to a tiny patch of Earth and time. I thought that it must seem very much like this when we focus on the dark end of the Light spectrum.

The play of Light allows us to see our Earthly world, ourselves, our creations. It is like the beam of a flashlight. At one end is full Light. As you move along the shaft, the Light gradually fades, until there is only darkness. Technically, there is no such thing as dark. Darkness is simply the absence of Light. In the dark, our choices are based on the limited view of our immediate vicinity, until the Light appears.

We humans have additional layers of being that give us different options. The colors in this dream-vision ran the spectrum of light to dark, but with all the combinations in between. We can travel through the entire range of combinations based on our personal choices. The result of these choices over time has been a layering of rules upon rules and words upon words that create never-ending requirements for more and more of the same. It is like replaying a scene over and over. It becomes locked like cement in our subconscious.

What we hold in our subconscious becomes a belief that is re-created in form over and over. Therefore, we roll through the ages of our world re-cycling the same choices and ultimately achieving the very same outcomes, albeit within different scenarios. By always believing ourselves to be locked within the Light to the dark spectrum, we are maintaining the predictable play of our collective lives. When we all cease to buy into this polarity-duality illusion, it will end.

There is another choice. There is a power that transcends all Earthly barriers to the realm of our Source. Outside our dimension, there is no polarity or duality. The key is to leap above and beyond what we think we know, to open our beliefs just a crack and take a closer look at the unknown. Jump off the see-saw and do not get back on.

Our reality within this dimension is not absolute. It is limited only by what we believe it to be. Human minds demand that all things contain a beginning and an end, carry a label of good or bad, create a choice of Light or dark and sometimes a grey spot on the spectrum in between, because these are easily perceptible in three-dimensions.

The Source Light that our heart translates into Rays illuminates the vast spectrum of frequencies that exists beyond our comprehension of Light and dark. It is the only power that overrules the polarity-duality game. It erases the principle of cause and effect.

For when our intent lies within the Rays of Love, the response is the creation of more Love. No more ping-ponging back and forth, Light or dark, good or evil, peace or war. Only more and more wonder, respect, benevolence, purity, integrity, impeccability, and honesty are expanding us to a state where we will never have to decide to choose the Light. It will be the only essence we know.

This Light of Source is its delight in its creations. It is a delight-love that transcends anything we can comprehend. It has no duality or opposing force, no variation, no fractal or fragment to be recalled, no opposite realities to be harmonized, no other beings to be interfaced with. It is an essence which exists simply for the delight of existing —love for Love's sake.

This Love is not the love that we practice here on Earth. The polarity-duality principles of our dimension form our human understanding of love. Therefore, its opposite also exists. We cannot change this anymore than we can change the law of gravity. In human love, this translates into an unconscious expectation of return. We pour love into our children, and we expect that they will believe our practices, religions, do what we think is best for them and become upstanding humans— like us! And, of course, we expect they will love us back.

We fall in love, which is to say that we decide to extend our love to a person or thing. This is an enormous decision for us; therefore, we subconsciously expect something in exchange, a return on our investment, at the very least an expression of gratitude. We love that cute house on the beach and therefore create the expectation that those bricks and mortar will withstand everything nature throws at it simply because we pour so much of our loving energy into it. If the bricks fall apart, then it is someone else's fault— the building inspector, the cement manufacturer, the zoning-laws, the government, climate change. These examples are simply the natural laws of our dimension at work. This is not love, but a mutually agreed upon barter system.

Love for Love's sake is to love with no

expectation of return. Love for Love's sake accepts and allows the thing it loves to be as it is in its true nature— and still pours its love into it. Each of us is desperately, and mostly unconsciously, searching for the sensation of this Love. As a baby seeks its mother's arms, we instinctively seek the dimension where Love governs all. This is where our Soul came from and where it wants to return.

Practicing Love for Love's sake means going to our inner sun and floating with our Soul simply to sense this Love-Light wash through us, flood us. It is not necessary to create a modality or movement or unique structure or system. It is not something that can be translated into words or taught. It must be experienced and sensed in our hearts. This Love is already inside us. It is the beam from our Source. It talks to us through our Soul.

To live in this Love means it is immaterial to us whether the Earth turns purple and is populated by eight-legged creatures. All these would be the same for us because all we would see is the

Light of Source that is each other's essence. If we create from this Love-Light and the Earth turns purple, it is beautiful and elegant because it was created by Love for Love's sake. Consistently nurturing Love saturates our subconscious so that all our actions, conscious or otherwise, are for our highest good and for all around us.

Our heart is the portal for this Love, where we disarm our dysfunctional patterns and games, not by attempting to untangle the patterns through repetition, but by leaping right off the see-saw. By no longer recognizing it as a see-saw, but just a piece of wood. Superheroes will not miraculously appear to save us and wrench our planet back to its Light.

Transformation happens through each of us, individually. We then remember and can answer the call of the Light. We are the only kale-smoothie-drinking-Superheroes who can choose Love for Love's sake to save our world.

Conscious intention and clear, balanced thought will only take us so far. In the essence of Love for Love's sake, we don't need cognitive, emotional, or physical understanding or experience. We are beyond the need to define what no harm to others means. We no longer need to contemplate that we are all connected. We know we are. We are the essence. It would be unnatural and painful for us to act outside of our true nature; therefore, we cannot even imagine doing so. We know that what is in us is in all. Every impulse to 'do what I want' becomes 'do what I am.'

If I am Love for Love's sake, the frequency of this is pure. We experience it as wonder, respect, benevolence, absolute integrity, impeccability and honesty, and the infinity of other Rays of Light available to us. These are human-sized glimpses of the unity that we knew when we dwelled with our Source —a complete communion with a Love that has no separation, no conflict, no expectations.

As humans, we have the habit of choosing to

dwell in a particular preferred state. Each day we believe we are in a peaceful state or a sad state or an irritated state, and we choose our actions based on that. Even if we can maintain a state of the highest bliss and joy, we are still split in two. We are identifying with "this" versus "that." Opposing forces, perpetuating duality. This continues to create and maintain conflict within us at some level. Even if only slight, this conflict shadows the Light of our true essence.

In practical terms, we want to let go of defining ourselves in ways that take sides. When we yearn for heaven instead of Earth. When we smile at remembered bliss from our yoga class and then frown angrily at the person or pile of work in front of us, disturbing our peace; when we awaken to the lightness of our spirit, then catch a glimpse of ourselves in the mirror and comment negatively on the denseness of our body. When we smooth out our forehead wrinkles so beautifully during meditation then negatively refocus on the age lines around our mouth! Let go of defining ourselves at all, and we find the path to oneness with our Source.

Magical oneness is inside us, accessible all the time, waiting for us to tap into it and live within it. Once I viscerally experienced this, a calm pervaded my entire body and all its cells, because there was nothing more to prove, no more extraneous calculation, rationalization, intellectual or egoic muscle-flexing. When any of this arises from past habits, it takes only a quick moment of refocusing to clear it away.

Love for Love's sake is the only power that transcends all Earthly barriers, to transport us to our Source. Choosing to dwell in Light creates a massive ripple effect for all time, both for us and for all who are, ever have been or ever will be, connected to us. This Love is not something we bestow on our self or others; it is our very essence. Love is the beating heart of all creation. We are the beating heart of creation. Our hearts beat in unison.

I dreamed I was on a stone plateau high *above the valley floor. A massive plate of smooth, grey rock was cool beneath my bare feet. The rock emitted no vibration or frequency that I could sense. I was touching it, yet I felt suspended at the same time.*

The plateau was strangely silent, with not a single creature in sight. It was a bit odd but peaceful. I stood watchful and waiting.

Nothing was happening. After what seemed like some time, with curiosity and a touch of impatience, I slowly turned in a circle. Triggered by my movement, a collage of pyramid shapes shimmered into view all around me.

I approached, and a door appeared on the face of each pyramid. I stepped through the nearest one only to be stopped by a rock wall. I went to the next and again found a rock wall. I went in and out like this through several more.

Finally, I entered one and found myself in a corridor of sorts. An endless hall was filled with overlapping pyramid-shaped doors as far as I could see and into infinity. These doors opened effortlessly, beckoning with their secrets.

In delight, I skipped along this fascinating pathway, exploring the first one and then another and another, reveling in the treasures I found on the other side.

8

Entering the Prism

Our sole purpose in life is Soul. We are conditioned to believe the Soul is some mystical, mysterious substance, or a distant, separate entity with which only the initiated can have a relationship. In truth, it is our buddy, our closest companion. We do not wait to meet our Soul after death; we encounter it in life. It lives intimately tucked within and around our body for our entire experience from the first cell to the last breath!

Our body is but a temporary shell fashioned to encase it while we live on Earth. Our Soul animates this shell, bringing to life tissues, bones, and organs. Having opened the door to a relationship with mine, I cannot for the life of me understand why I procrastinated for so long! It holds within it a world of fascinating information just waiting to be discovered, like all those pyramid doors opening to new worlds.

From our Soul, we know our authentic Self, as we currently like to call it. It is here in the Soul, within its blessed quiet, that we can hear that 'still, small voice' of Spirit, the Messenger of our Source, whispering our hope, reminding us to love and to trust.

Soul itself is just a placeholder. It is a word and concept developed to define that part of us that is not of this reality. Our ego fights to hang on to three-dimensional understandings, to language definitions, to the thing, the place, the time. To live in our Soul untethers us from the anchor of all that. Once we do so, we can ride our Soul out of this dimension to where our Light originated. From there, we bring back the riches of knowledge and wisdom to power us through our lives with grace and clarity of purpose.

When I sought my Soul, it was like going to another world, as in *The Lion, the Witch, and the Wardrobe* by C.S. Lewis. The wardrobe was the bridge between two worlds through which children passed back and forth for their adventures. In all descriptions of searching for the Soul connection, it appears there is a barrier that we each need to pass through within ourselves to be able to activate free access to our Soul and the Light consciously. This barrier is primarily our ego. It must be leaped over and relegated to its rightful place in our Soul-human life.

We could also visualize this as stepping back and forth between two parallel tracks. These tracks are not side-by-side parallel; instead, one set is inside the other. Remember jumping hopscotch as a child? Feet land wide on the outside squares, then hop and land on the inner squares. Two parallel tracks illustrate the concept of separation. Leaping from the outside to the inside track represents moving within. We cannot think our Self to the inside track. It requires a leap-hop of faith and the experience of the heart sensation that lands us there.

Our inner sun-heart is the portal to the Light. It can be opened or closed by us at the command of our will (the bottom point of the diamond). To sense this, it helped me to visualize my heart as a container with an opening in the front and the back. Though not anatomically correct, this image brought my mind under control to explore and lock onto the sensations I needed to feel to connect to this portal.

The back opens to Source Light. That side of the container is always open, and the Light is always accessible by our Soul. The front opening allows the Rays from the prism to project into the world. In between the back and the front I suggest you visualize a little gate that swings in both directions and acts as the prism.

Our job is to open the gate and let our human self merge with this Light. Each time we consciously shift to our heart, we open this gate a little wider. The more we shift, the more it opens, the larger the prism becomes, and the more Light floods through it. It is like a vast container within our center, a wormhole to another reality designed to attract like a magnet ever-increasing amounts of Light.

The first time I reached this space, it seemed empty, yet it was clear there was something there. It was filled with an essence that I could not identify. Scientists have not yet been able to determine what comprises the universe. I recently read somewhere that science has identified only 4% of what is out there.

The sensation of reaching this space was like going back into the womb, tunneling up and out the other end—a bit like the reverse of being born. I felt as if I was wriggling back through the birth canal into a tinier skin suit, then shrinking until there were no physical cells left at which point, I popped right out of myself. I was back to being the filament of my Soul, looking around in wonder at the universe. For those with female anatomy, it might be easier to imagine as we have the physical sense of open space (the womb) within us that connects to the external world. For those with male anatomy, perhaps it might help to remember that at one time you traveled that route at birth. There is a cellular memory of that.

Another option is to choose the navel point, where our umbilical cord once attached us to the open space of the womb. In addition to its physical function, the navel is also a powerful two-way energy portal unifying us with all other forms of life. As the bottom point of the diamond, we can use it to travel inwards and upwards through the solar plexus area to the heart.

Accessing Source Light is a metaphysical journey. We cannot physically reverse ourselves back through the womb, or the navel, of course. We travel this route by intending our consciousness to do so and believing it can and will.

In meditation, we are taught to go to the quiet center within us. Many sense this as a calm, peaceful place, a passive place, and it is lovely to rest there. First, we learn how to quiet our minds, bodies, and nervous systems. Then we learn to hold this quiet for extended periods. Then we learn to listen to the hum within us that is our Soul. Then we discover we can dialogue with it. It is somewhat like tuning to a radio bandwidth. After a bit of practice, we find our frequency.

The next step is understanding that this inner space does not always have to be passive. It is also a two-way portal with which we can actively engage, to give and receive Light from Source. We can consciously open it to draw in more and more Light. To me, this feels like I am a hollow tube with a thin outer shell. My inner space is the hollow tube. This hollow is not empty but filled with my Soul and masses of light frequencies surrounded by my thin, transparent shell of a body. Now I am a substantially-sized person. My body is in no way transparent. It is very, very solid!

Here I am speaking of the world of sensation, feeling, and vibratory frequencies.

Another way of sensing this is to visualize an oak barrel. Our physical body is the oak outer shell of the barrel. The open space within the barrel is our Soul. The more I connect with my Soul and my Light, the more the oak barrier feels thinner and thinner until it seems almost transparent. My Soul life and my human life then merge to be one.

I fully understand how difficult this may be for many to wrap their mind around. It was challenging for me until I stopped thinking about it, shut off the chatter of my mind, and practiced merely floating in the sensation. The journey is not of the mind, or any other structure, principle or law of our Earth dimension. We find our destination by looking way beyond our current perspective, beyond the comforting safety of logic and science to the realm of "what if," to acknowledge that we do not know what we do not know.

Finding our Light does not take us to a place; it takes us to a moment. A trip to the Light can happen in the blink of an eye. The knowledge received there is instant and vast.

In the Hollywood movie, *Contact*, the lead character travels to another dimension and returns. In human time it took only a few minutes, and everyone thought the mission unsuccessful. The woman claimed that she talked with someone in that other dimension for hours. She was disbelieved. However, after the scientists had moved on, a tape recorder was discovered. She had carried it with her during her mission. During the few short minutes of Earth time that she was seemingly gone, the tape had recorded hours of sound. Physically she moved nowhere. But her heart's conviction allowed her consciousness to travel to a specific place and stay there for hours, which recorded as hours of white noise on her tape machine.

Our intention is one of the most powerful tools in our toolbox. It is the intention and the depth of belief underlying that intention that allows us to transition beyond our human dimensions to our Soul. While all these images of barrels and wombs and navels are helpful, they are simply tools to assist our rational faculties in letting go and allowing our intention to work its magic. The biggest secret hiding in plain sight is that whatever we intend—with the conviction of heart-Light-Love—will come to pass. It happens all the time.

It is thought-provoking to realize that everything we do begins with an intention, conscious or otherwise. I intend to type a word, and instantly, my nerves and muscles fire up, ready to tap the keyboard, before my hand begins to move. I plan to stand up, and my muscles are tensed in readiness before my mind gives the command to act physically. When we believe we can travel to inner space and then intend it to happen, it will. It may take some practice to hold the intention steadily, but once learned, it happens.

Years ago, I was visiting a shaman healer to figure out what was going on with my heart. I was having the physical sensations of angina, yet medically all was fine. She held her hand over my heart, told me there was a shadow there, and then she pulled it out. I instantly felt such lightness of being. It was as if someone had blown a cool breeze through my chest, and it was open and free.

She told me she was demonstrating a point and would have to put the shadow back as it was my job to figure out why it was there and how to take it away. I was not happy about that! To try and illustrate this for me, she asked me to move my consciousness from my mind, where it typically dwelled, into my heart to search for the answer. Right then and there, with her watching. I felt like I was back in school, performing a test before the teacher, such was my ego.

I obediently quieted my breathing and then

focused my inner vision within my head as if there was a ball there. I mentally grabbed the ball and moved it downwards. I thought I had it, so I opened my eyes and looked at her expecting to receive my gold star. She smiled kindly and said, "Well, it is about half-way down your throat, not quite in your heart." My pride was stung! More practice required.

Sometime later, I was in a situation with one of my sons. He had done something disrespectful, not for the first time, and so I was confronting him toe-to-toe, ready to pour forth the same response I usually offered. An emotional response filled with emotional frustration and the usual phrases: "You know this is not allowed, how many times will you keep doing this, one of these days you will truly cross the line, etc., etc." The typical parent-child dance.

Before the words left my mouth, I noticed that my head was full of heat, like an overheating car radiator. The next second, this heat dropped with a plop into my heart. The subsequent outpouring of words from my heart was very different, very brief, and Soul-to-Soul such that he had no response. The dance was over. I remember turning quickly away and heading to my meditation room. I sat in stillness and in wonder at how easily I had slipped into my heart space and how different my response had been.

I took the time to memorize the sensation of dropping easily into my heart. That was what I had been searching for without realizing it, the sensation of how it felt physically. I needed to remember that sensation follows intention, just as our muscles contract *after* we set our intention to move. Shifting into my heart space was a total shifting of my center of gravity. It was like the rock in my dream-vision. I was standing yet suspended; in the world but not attached to it. After more practice, I was able to move my consciousness around freely and easily within my heart space to my Soul and my Light. I have never again felt chained to the mental constructs of this world unless I intentionally will it so.

There is such delight in exploring the facets of our Soul and anything else to be found in there! The pyramids in the dream-vision were nudging me to the sensation of skipping down that corridor and opening the doors to the fascinating stuff on the other side.

Focusing more and more on our inner planes where we find our Light merges our internal and external planes to oneness. I can live in my inner space because it is also one with my outer surrounding space. I can live in my outer space because it is one with my internal space. As within, so without.

Our Soul-heart connection is the portal. To walk through this portal does not mean that we will leave this Earth, leave our families, our career, or give up our favorite toys! It merely means that we can balance the relevance of all of that. Our significance as a human does not lie in the physical trappings of life, the stuff that is 'out there.' It pulses within us, in our Soul.

*I **dreamed*** *I was in a mystical place where everything shimmered with rainbow-like frequencies of never-before-seen colors overlapping and dancing.*

Gradually the colors at the center of this ethereal scrim coalesced into the form of a blindingly-white Shining One, tall and majestic and benevolently stern.

He gestured left toward a table where sat a book that was ancient, well-worn, and very thick. He held out his hand, and I passed him a sizeable old-fashioned gold key, which had suddenly materialized out of nowhere. He took the key, unlocked the clasp, and opened the book to a specific page.

He beckoned me forward to look into that page. The instant I did, Light blazed all around us. He said, "This is you. When we of the other realms and dimensions look through the veils at you, this is what we see."

He said, "There is no shadow; it is an illusion of what exists when Light is not shining. Where Light is not, there is only a void of Light. There are no evil energies or monstrous creatures. There is nothing to fear there. Humans have created the illusion of evil lurking in the shadows through the imaginative power of thoughts over the long years of its existence."

"Look through the eyes of a child."

"Look with the Light of wonder and single focus. Where a child looks, it focuses all its senses, and it sees only the thing that is present. When a child shifts its focus, the place of its prior focus ceases to exist for it. Where they do not look, nothing exists. As children grow and begin to share the group memories of the Earth realm, they begin to see illusions in the darkness."

"Shine the full strength of your Light, and there will no longer be shadow or fear."

9

Dancing Around the Light

I create a beautiful icing over a cake of shit –
pardon the language! A dear friend spoke these
words to me. I love her that she cared enough to
say this to my face. At the time, I believed I was
creating the best version of myself, both inter-
nally and externally. I had thought my insides
were matching my outsides. I had been working hard to clear my fears and my shadows, to
release the remnant energies of my past, gather
its wisdom, and move forward in Light.

Despite all this work, many physical, mental,

and emotional issues still plagued me so that I felt as if nothing was clearing at all, for surely it would start to show somewhere! I confess her words rocked me to my core. I chose to heed them and look at this process from another perspective.

The issue was that I could not keep a stable inner sun. In other words, I could not keep a consistent connection to my inner Light and my Soul. All those shadows and stories, memories, and traumas seemed so essential to hold. This stuff had to go so I could have a beautiful icing over a beautiful cake.

Harmony. The Soul-cake and the human-icing. Two separate entities. Our sole purpose is to harmonize our Soul agenda with our human (physical) plan. Our three-dimensional human form provides our Soul the means to experience and create. Constant separation of these two blocks this creation experience and can often replace it with never-ending cycles of self-sabotage.

So often, we do not know why we self-sabotage. And it is not because we have no willpower to give up the taste of indulgence! What often underlies this behavior is "if I cannot find my Soul, then I will indulge everything else that this human life offers." Of course, this is more unconscious than conscious. The result is living in a kind of haze, neither with our Soul nor entirely without our Soul. Shadows and fears are created by cloaking ourselves in ignorance of this essential connection.

Lighting Up the Shadows

Shadow is a reflection of the light. It is neither light nor dark, nor half-light. It is a blocked light that manifests as an unsteady apparition of that which is blocked.

A healer once told me shadows were skipping around my heart. These were shadows of my own making. Once I let these go, the Light would be full, and I would have access to all the wonders that would bring. She further explained that once the Light is fully flowing from our hearts, we believe our work is complete. We think we have reached our goal. We have arrived at the finish line, and there is nothing more to do.

Once we let this Light shine fully, it is only the beginning. From this point, the Light gets brighter and stronger. Even the greatest imaginations cannot conceive of the experiences we will have with it.

I was skeptical. I questioned the need for releasing all this stuff. I was born this way, and that is just who I am. I was generally okay and relatively content. Her response was to question why I would want to live a half-life, a relatively happy life when I could live a delighted life. Put like that, I had no smart comeback!

I do believe that it is healthy to excavate what lies in our personal shadow kingdom. To open our particular Pandora's Box. The hardest part is our first foray into our shadows. The protocols used in shamanic ceremonies and similar methods are, to me, the most effective and efficient of all the paths to this type of healing.

These protocols go beyond the mental and emotional understanding of trauma to healing the Soul-human connection. Going even further, they transform the energy of trauma by clearing its residue from deep within our cells. This also clears the Earth's field and ripples out to our ancestors and descendants and returns to our Source. This type of healing is instant and profound; a fast-forward that can be intense and exhausting, but joyfully rewarding. I would highly recommend it!

My first foray into my shadow self was horrible. Rest assured it gets a little more comfortable the more we clear. For years since my heart attack, I had strange angina-like pain that was not traceable on medical technologies. Recall that session I mentioned previously when the shaman pulled the dark energy out of my heart to show me that the pain was energetic and not physical. I had felt so light! After she put the shadow back, she gave me some tips on where to start the healing process, and I went home to meditate on this.

What happened next scared the 'you know what' out of me so much that I had to return to see her the next day. My visions tend to be vividly alive as that is the quickest way messages get through to me. In this meditation, a black panther appeared, told me to hop on its back, and proceeded to race down a long tunnel to the middle of the Earth, or so it seemed.

A huge Shining One met us at the point between sky and earth and stationed itself there in a protective stance. My panther fought off all manner of dark shadowy creatures on the way down through the blackness until we landed on the rocky floor of what appeared to be a cave. He gently tipped me off and nudged me to the far corner.

In that corner was a woman presiding over the bones of many dead and rotten bodies. With a start, I realized I was looking at a mirror image of myself. When I made eye contact with this creature woman, a voice tolled in my head: "You kill things." These were the bones of my kills. Well, I jumped back on the panther and ordered him up and out. I ripped myself back to reality, opened my eyes, retching in horror. What did that mean—I kill things—present tense? Those bones were from people!

Despite the emotional drama elicited by the vision, it did sort itself out to be the shadow on my heart. It causes me to hoard my love which I then mete out incrementally whenever I choose to—or not. Through this action, I sometimes kill another's love for me. I can lash out and slay someone with the sharp edge of my tongue. I can throw lightning bolts from my eyes with a single look. I can turn away in indifference and wither any kind thoughts in another.

This indifference pattern was the most heart-wrenching for me to accept. I never thought this was part of my character, yet I came to see how it can mask itself in subtle ways, like watching someone trip on the sidewalk. Instead of going over to see if they are okay, we watch from a distance to be sure they are back on their feet. We tell ourselves we helped by being there if needed. Yet the real help would have been our love frequency pulsed to that person if we had walked over and given them our arm to help them up.

All of these are perversions of the heart energy. The Light Rays can be manipulated by deliberately opening and closing the portal of our heart. Once I excavated this concept from deep within myself, I was able to embrace that shadow, in the form of that mirror image of me in the bone cave. I understand why my Shadow Self was with me, what caused this, what she needs from me, and what she takes from me. She will always be a part of me, yet through my taking responsibility and accepting this part of myself, she can rest at peace within me. This shadow is no longer a shadow.

Taking that first step into (and out of) our shadows places us in territory that feels unstable and unpredictable. If you choose to do this work, I highly recommend finding someone who has been in that place, a lamplighter who can shine the Light on that first step and walk beside you till you get your bearings.

If we want to, we can focus continually on our shadows, but there comes the point when it is time to move on from dissecting the details, remain mindful of the major themes and focus on the wisdom acquired. Key is to acknowledge that we have shadows and that they are as beautiful to us as all our other aspects. This is when we master the art of gentleness with Self—softness in allowing our Self to love and let go.

We can acknowledge the Shadows that may continue to dance around us without attachment. Once they are loved, they have no power left to harm. If they surface randomly in my thoughts and actions, I say hello to them, acknowledge them and enfold them in my Light with respect. In the Light from our Soul, they no longer control us—we manage them. Eventually, these shadows and their triggers cease to exist. Our reality transforms because we are creating a different one without the shadows.

Shadows are thoughts and actions that do not stem from our Light. In the Light, we can see all the angles and dimensions of them. We notice every time we act without wonder, respect, benevolence, purity, integrity, impeccability, honesty, and, so on. The shadow shows itself to be just one element of our Self that vibrates at a different frequency.

It is an out-of-tune melody that simply requires a little re-tuning to harmonize with us once again. Shadow-work is, in essence, emptying ourselves of our history to create room for a new story.

Half-light

There is only one way to extinguish our Light, and that is to die physically. When our body shuts down, our Soul returns to its origin, and our Light leaves this world. However, in our life here before that event, we can come very close to extinguishing our Light, by covering it with a dense blanket of greyness. This is zombie-land, the land of the half-light, neither in full Light nor the complete absence of Light. Here we are disconnected fragments of the Soul-human being. In a sense, we are imposters.

Here we do not commit to either light or dark so we can slide a little either way at will. We do not stand out. We blend in. No one can find fault with us either way. We believe this is the safest place to live. In this land, suffering is often self-inflicted by choosing apathy and willful ignorance, by being deliberately unaware or neglectful. The Rays cannot manifest in the half-light. They become a bit stunted. It may appear we are manifesting them, but they are in a watered-down strength. Holding half-respect for something is neither respect nor non-respect. Half wonder is not wonder at all.

Arguably one of the most harmful manifestations of a half-light life is the current trend to spend hours sponging up the soul-numbing goo of movies, video games, you-tube stunts, and overblown newscasts. In the half-light, we justify numbing ourselves with substances like alcohol, prescription, and recreational drugs, or even sugar, not to feel the depths of our shadows. We can watch mass horror being perpetrated on movie screens (oh, but it is not real!), or personally perpetuate those same horrors through video games (oh, but it is not real!).

We live vicariously through all the nasties of the seven deadly sins—pride, lust, sloth, greed, envy, wrath, gluttony—thinking this will have no impact on us. All of which reinforces our understanding of a reality where there is an "us and them," a bad guy and a good guy, superheroes and imperfect, insignificant little humans, and of course, it reinforces our belief that we are powerless.

There are similar dangers inherent in a lifetime spent 'blissing out' in commercial-style yoga classes or mass religions, believing we have attained enlightenment. My heart is joyful for those who feel they hold an enlightened state. Yet I wonder how many of us, in reality, have simply attained a sense of surface calm which holds us aloof from the sufferings of others and boxes in our own fears and tucks them away.

We may think we have earned the Universe's permission to ignore those who suffer, simply because they do not follow our belief systems.

Looking back, I can see how I lived a half-light life for many years. I was a two-dimensional human masquerading as a fully functioning three-dimensional being. I was fully productive, effective, and efficient. Full of action and forward movement. Yet there was a void under this façade.

Decades ago, I reached a point of collapse. I woke up after a suicide attempt and vowed to myself that nothing and no one would drive me to that point ever again. I promised to protect my inner self and my energy field, and the vow implied—at any cost. Be careful what promises you make with yourself! At that time, I did not know what I was setting in motion as I was not yet consciously versed in the principles of intention and energy. The power of that vow set in motion massive ripple effects within me that resulted in erecting an impenetrable barrier around my heart.

During those years, I was close to a cousin who was decades older than me and an ordained minister. He was a rather unorthodox minister, a rough and tumble kind of guy, yet he understood the concept of love. He passed to me one of the wisest messages of my life. When I was struggling to know how I had gotten to where I was and how I was going to move forward, he said to me, "It is not possible to shut down your love for one, without shutting down your love for all."

I did not believe him, of course! I always felt that whatever I put my mind to, I could do. So, I proceeded to live like a chameleon, shape-shifting as required for the next decade. Remember the heart shadow and the lady in the cave of bones?

My cousin was right. We cannot split our hearts in that manner. It is not possible within the structure of our Soul and its Light to do so without serious consequences to our physical self. I would learn this the hard way, as finally, my physical heart could no longer sustain the pressure. A major heart attack was the result of years of willfully depriving myself of the natural flow of Light and love and convincing myself this was the safest way to survive.

At the apex of the attack, when the muscle stopped contracting, and there was no more oxygen incoming, I settled into a lovely state of calm. To the outside world, I was unconscious, grey-colored, and not breathing. Inside I was on the most beautiful journey of my human consciousness.

I traveled up through a large, wormhole-like space to a wide-open light that waited at the end. I passed through the light portal into another dimension out of time.

There were Shining Ones there, waiting for me. They showed me my life. Not a past life review, a fast-forward life teaser. They showed me what my life could be if I chose to return to my body. What I experienced was not a series of places, or people, or situations. It was a feeling, a Light, an essence. They showed me how I would feel within my human body if I returned and connected to my Soul and the Light of Source.

I can't put this feeling into words. Peace, bliss, serenity, joy, and more, of proportions and frequencies not of this Earth. Then came a brief flash of life events as they would be when steeped in this frequency. It was a tiny taste of oneness with Source.

I returned to this world inspired but grieving for the loss of that feeling. It took time, but I found it again within my heart and with my

Soul. I wonder now how we can ever honestly believe we can live without this essence of our Source that is such a perfect Love. Choosing the half-light robs us of such joy and richness of experience.

Absence of Light

Fear is the absence of Light, the absence of love. It is not the opposite of love. Fear does not exist as its own essence. It is a response, a reaction. It flares up when we suppress our Light and turn away from our Source.

Fear is a projection of the past (memory) or future (imagination). The past and future do not exist. There is only the moment we are in. At that moment, all that truly exists for us is choice. Will we choose the remnant emotion of a past memory? Will we choose a fanciful concoction of our wildly creative imagination? Or will we choose to remain in the moment and deliberate only upon the facts present at that moment?

Fear is a response. It shows up when we have an issue to work through. It is often our first response, a reflection of the fight or flight instinct triggering us to stop and look. The mind alone cannot resolve fear. We are capable of manufacturing all sorts of mental scenarios to explain our thought patterns and behaviors. This creates a false perception of security. When we brush up against the perimeter of this perceived security, it dissolves, and we create more fear. To banish our fear, we must move to our Light. At one point on my journey, I had a lovely guru tell me that I read too many books and took too many courses – one of which was his! He kindly told me that while all this information gathering was valuable to a point, I needed the real work in my heart! This inner work is not a function of the mind. It is a visceral experience with our Light and our Soul. At the time, I had no idea what he meant, but his words triggered the fear response. I honestly thought I was doing the inner work!

Fear is a form of resistance to the forces of

change and growth. It creates envy of others, anger at self, agitation, and looking over the shoulder for dark things. It is our fears that attract that darkness to us. Even seemingly insignificant things like saying, "I cannot drink alcohol, because my liver will collapse." The truth is that my liver does not feel comfortable with alcohol, so it gives me a little pain, which is telling me not to subject it to that substance. It is not telling me it is in a state of imminent collapse. What is happening is simply a fear surfacing from some distant memory - or too many pharmaceutical ad campaigns! It is not a truth. Yet if I keep thinking and saying that, it very well might manifest as one.

Fear is a form of restriction. When we place limits on ourselves that are not a function of support to our Soul path, we restrict the flow of our Light. This creates overwhelming pressure as we work to bring in more and more Light to overcome self-imposed barriers, yet it has no place to go. We will burst. I saw this concept as a bubble of white light. This bubble was my inner star of

Light, and in this vision, I saw it radiating about a foot all around me. There was a solid perimeter around the bubble, against which I was pushing to make the bubble larger so that my Light could radiate farther. This restrictive perimeter was my fear, which I had created by my dogmatic and overly structured black and white, linear, finite view of my world. I was attempting to bring in more Light-Love without releasing the fear. I was trying to cram more and more Light into this finite bubble, which was packing it so tightly that it became opaque, gel-like, and eventually stagnant. By releasing my perimeter of fear, the Light flowed outward to infinity. It became like a translucent veil that swayed, changed colors, and could be shaped and directed.

Fear disguises itself in tricky ways. It can manifest with subtle nuance. I came across a section in my journal from a wellness conference written years ago. The exercise was to write down all our self-limiting thoughts. I had written things like: Others might think me silly; something might go wrong due to my lousy judgment; my body cannot be trusted to support me; I do not have anything unique to say or do; what if I lose control and get into a situation I cannot get out of; I am old and fat and tired; it is too hard to try to make myself understood; I am too intense and scare people away. There were pages more! I had analyzed myself right down to the Nano-degrees! As I read back over all these, it was clear to me that there was only one thought I should have written. I am afraid.

Fear closes our hearts. We may tell ourselves this is a good, necessary thing. We do it so others cannot hurt or control us. We do it to keep the shadows out — the shadows of ourselves, our misuse of Light that we do not want to face. We fear we will break apart if we open up our heart and let in all the perceived pain. Closing our hearts is purposefully withholding our Light. It is a misuse of our power, a carelessness, a passive-aggressive action that creates harm — a negligent abuse of the most magical alchemy of all.

We fear the Light; this is the most remarkable concept to me. We fear the Light of which we are made! We fear to live fully in this Light. We fear to let go of our shadows and our darkness. Underlying this fear is the belief that we are not worthy of the Light. We worry because we do not know who we are. We fear that when we reach inside ourselves, there will be nothing there. We think we will implode. We command attention and feel valued by the substance of our external shell of beauty, brains, success. Some try to imitate another's path, or a reality TV show, or the values of a person who has 'got it all together.'

We fear to invite in more Light because then we will have to change. The Light needs room; therefore, it will push out all the other stuff we have piled up in our hearts and bodies. It is all energy frequency. Our bodies can only hold so much. Therefore, when we bring Light in, shadows must move out. As I sketched this section,

I was very emotional. I was not sure why or what this intensity was, at first. It soon was apparent that more Light was trying to expand within me. To do this, it pushed before it all the non-Light I was still holding. Rage! It became glaringly apparent that I was processing the last remnants of intense anger. This process reinforced my belief that not all that comes up for release requires a detailed review. Often there are left-over frequencies that we carry in our cells from events already healed. Such was my case.

I so buried my rage that I didn't recognize it as the emotion we associate with anger. In past years I had looked in detail at all the events that caused me outrage. I understood them; I conquered the triggers; my emotions were steady. The rage that was burrowed so deeply was non-specific, a collective rage. Yet it had never manifested as rage, so I did not even know it was there.

After it was healed and completely gone, I saw its pattern. It had found its way into my daily life in the form of adrenaline-fueled activity. Obsessive goal-setting, planning, the underlying force that kept me rushing to accomplish "things," to never, ever rest. I assumed this was normal. I was a type-A personality, a go-getter, one who finishes what she starts (but she starts so many things!), the perfect mother, wife, executive.

Life was supposed to be this way. I was not overly emotional. I seldom was angry with anyone (except myself!). Yet buried rage was providing this seething foundation of volcanic-like activity. How could I genuinely build my character, centered in Light and Love, with this shifting foundation?

All that rage that subconsciously fueled me is now gone. Immediately after the last of it was cleaned out, I walked around for a week or so wondering why I felt so empty and unfocused. Nature abhors a vacuum! The newly-emptied space had to be filled. It took clear communication with my Soul to understand that filling it was simple. Fill it with Light! That was why I opened that space in the first place! Our Soul knows everything about us, especially those things we do not realize we do not know! Replacing the rage with Light has changed me in ways I could never have imagined. Now I wonder why I was ever fearful at all!

Our Light is the only thing we will be accountable for when we reach the moment of our physical death, and our Soul moves out of our body.

It is not vital that we had thousands of friends, or made it to every family gathering, or followed every commandment or human-made rule and regulation of our culture. It is only essential that we have beamed our Light through all levels of our emotional, mental, and spiritual being to all with whom we have come into contact.

Not "was I productive," not even "was I loved," but "did I love, was I filled with Light, connected to my Creator, and did I unfailingly project my Light."

I dreamed I was at the edge of a large lake. Thousands of people of all ages and backgrounds were milling about enjoying the sun's warmth, picnicking under shady trees, swimming in the clear waters, laughing, relaxing and reveling in this wonderful time to be alive.

A woman was there with me enjoying the day. All of a sudden, the idyllic world began to fall apart. The water churned angrily and rose up over the shore. The warm breezes turned to cold, punishing winds. The rocks crumbled and tumbled into the lake. Ancient trees were wrenched from the ground.

All was chaos. People ran for shelter in a nearby cottage and huddled together for comfort. They watched in mounting fear as the natural world outside became more and more violent.

I was standing calmly off to one side looking out a window. I saw a massive, ship-type object crashing towards us. It was twisting tornado-like and spewing black clouds of destruction in its wake.

As it came ever closer, the woman with me crept silently up behind me. She looked ill as if her life force was being sucked out of her. She was fading quickly. I was surprised she was in such a state, not understanding what was happening to her.

She pulled at me and begged me to call off the wild force outside.

I calmly stepped outside, held up my arms, and commanded it to cease and leave this world – it felt like the most natural thing to do.

The force obeyed, and almost instantly, the natural world righted itself. The sun came out, the land stopped heaving, and everyone spilled out of the cottage to resume their play.

It was as if nothing had happened.

10

Keeping the Light

The word 'light' triggers an outpouring of the thousands of phrases we use containing it: to light a path, lamplight, light gives life, to see the light, illuminate, she is a bright light, and on and on. A keeper is one who nurtures, keeps something alive, watches, guards, takes responsibility for, maintains.

The word Lightkeeper conjures fanciful images of a lighthouse and its keeper, a person carrying a lantern, a light in a window on a stormy night, a communal fire in an ancient village, temples and priestesses tending the sacred flame, the Statue of Liberty holding her light aloft.

To keep the light essentially means to nurture it as a steward would. A steward is one who pays attention and notices all the needs and requirements that make a thing flourish. Before electric light was invented, the keeper of a lighthouse had to steward the flame by merely keeping an eye on it so that it would not go out. He had to nourish it with fuel so that it would always burn at a specific brightness. The keeper did not sit all day, staring at the flame. He simply turned his attention to it every so often, as he went about the business of maintaining the house that protects the flame.

The flame is our Light, the house is our body. To steward our Light quite simply means to focus our attention on it, know that it is there, spend some time daily turning our thoughts to it. Visualize it in our mind's eye. See it as a flame that is strong and steady, shimmering with all the colors of the rainbow.

The word nurture is another well-used word

which typically connotes an activity of indulgent time-out, a step off the treadmill of the daily grind, activities like a day at the spa, or lounging with a good book, some wine, and chocolates. These sustain our physical and mental selves to maintain the stamina to get up the next day and go right back to the business of our physical survival. We think we have done an essential thing for our health, and in part, this is true. Our constant source of vitality, though, is our life-force and that spins to us through our Light. Take a minute to explore how much time you devote each day to activities that sustain your human body and how much you dedicate to sustaining your Light.

Nurturing our Light means doing those things that cause our Soul, its conduit, to thrive and keep feeding us. For me, who spends long periods writing, and a host of other mental exercises, nurture is anything that is the opposite. A whole day of scrubbing floors is a respite from what I usually do. As I spend so much time with

157

my eyes focused mere inches in front of me at a book or computer, it is nurturing to simply raise my physical eyes and look far away toward an open field, as an example. Planting my bare feet on the cool soil and not moving nurtures my Soul. Turning my face to the Sun's heat nurtures my Soul. Sharing a giggle with a baby feeds my Light.

Our human journey follows the same patterns as all else in the universe. Expansion and contraction. It helps to become aware of the expansion and contraction, the ebb and flow phases of our life. In a contraction phase, our Light is still there, burning softly, maintaining, until the upcoming expansion phase. By remaining alert in our minds, open in our hearts and consciously observing, we will recognize these phases for what they are and not create undue stress thinking we have missed the boat. A different ship will come in on the next expansion tide. We will recognize it if we keep our Light shining and our heart open.

We are still human, after all. Despite the lofty

ideals we set for ourselves, we are still living in a world that functions on a set of three-dimensional laws and principles. There may be times when we think we have lost our Light, that it is dimmed by overwhelming circumstances, that it has become tiny and insufficient. At these times, it is even more important to put some attention into finding our Light. We expend much effort reviewing our perceived darkness, through self-criticism and self-judgment, through commenting upon and judging people and situations around us. To thrive, we need to spend equal time focusing inwards on our Light. If we find ourselves talking out loud to the frozen chickens in the grocery store, it is time for some inward focus!

This often takes the form of prayer, meditation, observation, or contemplation. Observation is the act of sitting with thoughts we think need to be reviewed and letting them ramble around in our brain of their own accord. Contemplation is a more directed review that focuses on the save, discard, or act process. Prayer is voicing a question and requesting a response, the act of speaking to Source. Meditation is creating internal silence to listen for messages coming in; Source speaking to us.

While all of these have an essential function, keeping the Light is a little different. It is a set of activities to nurture, nourish and steward, to keep our Light burning brightly and actively expanding.

Acknowledge Your Light

The act of acknowledging something brings it into being. It brings it up from the murky subconscious or the unformed imagination. It creates it as a thought that requires a form. This form necessitates us pondering and reflecting and ultimately making sense of it for ourselves. Through this process, it becomes something that is real and holds meaning for us.

A simple example can be found in a room full of people. As we walk from one end to the other, scanning the crowd, we pass collectives of people standing, sitting or milling about around us that resemble vague shadows. We do not focus on them; therefore, they hold no meaning for us. They are a blur of humanity, sort of real, but not. If we continue on our way out the door, without acknowledging a single individual for more than the blink of an eyelash, we will hold only the memory of a blurry group of two-leggeds, and within a short time will have forgotten much, if not all, about them.

Instead of walking by, let's stop in front of one. We notice the clothes, red hair, and sparkling green eyes. Their eyes are messaging our eyes, just as our mouths are speaking words, and our bodies are expressing emotions to each other. We have no choice now but to acknowledge that this is not just a two-legged human but a fellow Soul that is real and meaningful.

In the same way, once we stop to acknowledge the Light we have within us and notice its qualities, it becomes real and meaningful.

Dip into Infinity

Take a moment each day to dip into the diamond. Visualize the prism sun-heart, its Light and its Rays. It takes only a moment. It feels like pushing a reset button. It can be done anywhere, in a taxi, on a plane, in the washroom. When I was at university, I used to do this without realizing it! I would randomly head to a restroom, sit on the toilet seat in the quiet, breathe, relax my shoulders, and stabilize my core.

When learning to meditate, I experienced an image that helped me quickly dip into the quiet of my heart space. The image is of three levels of descent. Each leads through to the next, not actually downwards, more spiraling inwards.

The first I call Agitation and the image was of a squirrel running helter-skelter. This is the mind and body level of my Self doing what comes naturally, running 100 miles per hour. When this squirrel pops up, I visualize a crystal orb settling on this squirrel to capture and focus it.

The second level I call Calm, and the image is of a monk reading quietly within his private space, but someone keeps calling to him that he is wasting his time. This is my conditioning where the voices in my head say, "Be productive, get up, this is not useful."

The third level I call Serenity, and the image is of a deep, dark pool. Here I am a single eye swimming slowly around observing, only observing. This is my still point. At this point, I can physically sit forever, moving deeper and deeper into infinity to create, communicate, receive. The deeper I drift, the more my consciousness travels out the long wormhole away from this Earthly body and world to infinity.

Over time and with repeated effort, I became able to drop instantly into that still point. I do this several times a day to refocus on my Light.

When I am in a hurry or scattered, I still resort to this imagery to take me quickly to a place of stillness, if only for a few quick minutes to recharge. Knowing that this still point is always possible to find releases stress when I have moments that never seem to get past the agitated squirrel!

Be An Explorer

There is a wonderful story that sticks in my memory as a beautiful example of how to explore beyond our personal perception and collective memory. It is the story of an indigenous people's first contact with a European ship a very long time ago.

As the two peoples met on the shore, the indigenous men and women puzzled at how the Europeans had arrived on the water. They could see the small rowboat, which was similar to their watercraft, but they could not make out the large ship. They could not process and therefore could not see its image because European-style ocean-going vessels were not in their collective memory.

Finally, the Wise Elder focused intently on the waterline where the Captain was declaring there was a ship. He could just make out a slight indent in the water at the line of the ship's hull. The elder confirmed that there was indeed something on the water. As the Wise One was trained to explore the dimensions beyond Earth, he was able to transcend his collective memories and open himself to the unseen and the unknown.

To explore means to release the mental blocks that limit the imagination. Imposing blocks to our natural curiosity is, in fact, implying that we humans are an unintelligent species, incapable of understanding anything we cannot see with our eyes or feel with our fingertips. Sometimes we need to get out of our own way and let our intuitive flow open us to the joy of the unknown.

Our personal and collective human memory has stored perceptions based on thousands of years and millions of humans living through situations and events, generation after generation. We can add totally new perceptions to our collective consciousness. Make the assumption that there are dimensions beyond ours and elements within these dimensions that we cannot comprehend within our limited human perception. Accept that we do not know what we do not know.

In essence, we each choose our reality by what we allow ourselves to believe. We say perception is reality. In fact, my perception is my reality, and your perception is your reality. Seven billion people on this planet, therefore seven billion perceptions of reality all bumping up against each other.

Choosing to set concrete parameters around our beliefs of reality allows us to hold our awareness only within those parameters. This does not mean there is nothing more to explore and perceive. Examining what has so far limited us, believing in infinite possibility, is all it takes to perceive and experience the other frequencies that exist all around us.

I continuingly explore simply by remaining receptive to everything and anything. When I see, hear or read something, I look for any resonance within me, or a possibility that I cannot as yet fathom, and I simply let it sit. It does not mean that I agree with every strange thing or change my beliefs every few minutes. It means that I am comfortable soaking up anything new and allowing it to simmer and filter within me. As with the indigenous people and the ship. They discovered a new and fascinating thing by remaining open to possibility.

Manage Your Thoughts

Know that your thoughts are only thoughts. Our mind creates over 50,000 thoughts per day. Its job is to generate thoughts. It is our job to discern which ideas are worth dwelling upon. Those we choose to dwell upon tunnel into our subconscious where they become challenging to dig out. Such thoughts create form. This is one of the most powerful of alchemies.

Part of our thought-managing process is to notice how many thoughts are stemming from a past event or a future wish. There is no past or future, no matter how hard we try to keep the past alive through memories or predict a future through imaginings. There is only the moment we are in. There is only the choice of Light-Love or no Light-Love.

Thoughts are created by our mind; therefore, we can direct our mind to uncreate them. Whenever we have ideas that are not created from Light, go to the inner sun, the heart space, and visualize a globe of white light cleansing them. Check each dominant thought against the Rays and their meanings. Every time you notice a harmful thought, simply brush it away as you would a fly. Do not let it take root. Those thoughts filled with Light create Light in material form.

Imagine sitting at a dinner party and being the recipient of an unkind comment from a friend. Historically, this friend has never been cruel to you. But at this moment, the circumstances of her day have pushed her past the limits of her self-control. The comment is unintentional and lacks heartfelt conviction. Its face value to you, though, is unkind and you are hurt by it. You have two options.

Knowing your friend as you do, you could channel Light into your emotions, speak quietly to her later, empathize with her challenging day, exchange hugs and the whole thing would be brushed away like the fly I mentioned earlier and forgotten as if it never happened.

The alternate route is that you hold her comment and your hurt in focus long enough that it takes root and burrows deep. You and your friend are thus set up for a rocky road ahead. The longer you wait to address the memory of this incident, the greater an obstacle it becomes. It might even solidify into anger, when, in truth, it was an unintentional event in the long years of your relationship. What your friend really needed was a bit of your love.

Pay Attention

Train yourself to be aware of your surroundings. Notice when something feels a little unusual, stop and check it out. Determine if there is a need to act on it or disperse the energy of it. I was in a

First Nations museum store on Vancouver Island a few years ago. I walked through the store and saw nothing that was calling out for me to purchase, yet for 15 minutes, I kept walking around and around the aisles feeling strongly that I could not leave.

I was just about to leave thinking I had misread the signs when the clerk suddenly popped out from behind the counter. I was the only one in the store, so I did wonder why it took him that long to decide to talk to me. I quickly managed that ego thought so it would not color whatever encounter was about to take place. He did not offer me sales assistance but instead began talking about the weather, which was unusually cold and blustery.

The conversation quickly led to the energetic properties of weather, and he passed on to me the thoughts of his elders about the timing of world events, as they see it playing out in the weather systems around their formerly peaceful land.

This was a fascinating message for me and

very relevant to my spiritual explorations of that time. If I had not been attentive to the sensation that told me to stay in the store, if I had not managed my thoughts, if I had not been open to exploring, I would have missed a lovely human connection and a profound message.

Watch for Signs

There are always signposts throughout our journeys that tell us how we are doing or where to go next. Watch for signs, particularly when we are struggling and feel stuck. Sometimes we are actually finished working through something, the healing is done, yet the memory of it survives. Our Soul knows when it is time to release the memories of that struggle as they no longer serve.

Perhaps we have turned a major corner on our journey, and the Universe wants us to step forward with joy to the next plateau, yet we think we are still approaching that corner. Sometimes our Light is shining brighter than we think it is and we are being prompted to let it fly free.

I left my corporate career at the age of 50, with no plans. Life was an open road! I signed up for yoga teacher training at the urging of a friend. This was not what I had thought the open road would look like, but I needed something to do until I figured that out. It turned out to be the catalyst for a seven-year journey to unbury my Light and reacquaint my human self with my Soul self.

The first night of the first weekend of study, I had a curious dream. Let me preface this by saying that up until that weekend, I never remembered my dreams unless they were horrible nightmares, and these did not come often. Each night of my life to that point was a deep, dreamless, uneventful sleep. Therefore, this dream was all the more intriguing. It was a linear story, not at all scary, and I remembered every bit of it when I woke up!

The dream was an amalgamation of several nightmares from my teen and early adult years. This night, the situations had been turned into a gentle linked progression with a lovely ending for all involved. It was a crystal-clear sign that the segment of my life related to those fears was done. It was a resolution-release-and-move-on type of dream. It was one of the most beautiful manifestations. To this day, I remember every detail of this dream, and the memory fills me with peace.

Sometimes a sign is lightning quick. My husband and I were on a road trip years ago through the lands of the Acadian people in the Maritimes of Canada. In companionable silence, we were enjoying the scenery flying by outside the truck. We passed a sign for a village called St. Joseph du Moine.

Suddenly I was shifted outside of myself, and there was an apparition of a monk hovering in front of me. Moine, from the town's name, means monk in the French language. He bathed my face in water, lifted his hand in blessing, and left. It happened so unexpectedly, and so quickly that I was quite startled.

I checked the clock on the truck. No time had passed. My husband had seen nothing. However,

I felt a blissful reassurance within me, for which I thanked the monk who must surely have been the locally renowned St. Joseph.

These types of signs happen more often than we realize, and they are not random or coincidental. They are assistance sent to us when we need it. They bring a measure of peace to our journeys and a lovely boost of Light.

Check for Blind Spots

There are times that we connect, we know, we hear and see clearly, yet we decide to ignore. This willful blindness is a significant cause for concern as it cements patterns of behavior. We all have blind spots, and these are usually areas we do not want to acknowledge. When we say something like "I just cannot believe he said that to me, or did that to us," or "that will never happen to me," and so on, these are manifestations of blind spots.

Our ego believes it knows best, and we should only listen to it. Believing that thing will never happen to me is the height of egotistical arrogance. Anything can happen to anyone. None of us are immune to being human. The patterns of our blind spots can manifest in a variety of situations, but the underlying issue will be the same. These are the times our Soul nudges us strongly to see our truth.

Several years ago, I was on one of my lovely road trips to a little town for a Gem and Mineral Show. It was one of the oldest shows in North America but also one of the smallest in vendor attendance, so not logically worth it for the effort involved to get there. Thinking rationally, I had lots of crystals and did not need to purchase any more.

Yet I felt so compelled to be there, that we trundled our way down a bumpy old highway to the detriment of our rig, ending up camped in a tiny little spit of a campsite, with another hour to drive the next day to get to the show.

One of my blind spots is speed! I am blessed with a lightning-quick mental comprehension.

This can also be a challenge, as I tend to act with the same lightning speed. Between understanding and action, many steps really should be inserted! I have to consciously make myself stop and reflect at all times.

It is also a matter of trust in the Soul, and at the time of this incident, I was still working on that! When we consciously stop to reflect, we open the space for our Soul to engage us in conversation. A far more meaningful and appropriate action will, therefore, follow.

At the show, I was blindly walking around, compulsively buying up stones I did not need like a puppet on a string wondering what was going on. While taking another speedy turn around the floor, a woman suddenly stepped right into my path, nose-to-nose with me, forcing me to either stop or run her over. She looked at the crystal I was wearing around my neck, stuck her face inches from mine, and aggressively said, "That is a pretty stone. I personally use a Smoky Quartz crystal for healing." She then spun and disappeared back into the crowd. She did not smile, say hello, or goodbye. In fact, she was rather fierce! I did not see where she came from or where she went. I searched the crowds. There was no trace of her. Vanished!

Clearly, this strange encounter was why I was there. There was a transfer of elemental energies from the woman to me that could only happen at that place, on that rock, beside that body of water.

Another of my blind spots has to do with the land we inhabit. Powerful currents run through every part of our Earth. They resonate differently within different people and at different times. The call of the land is a part of me that I have ignored for decades as I raced through life. On this trip, I was magnetically pulled to this exact plot of earth, yet I questioned and grumbled all the way.

Another of my blind spots is how I respond to such events. Typically, I would think the woman was crazy, the encounter was weird and dismiss it, which I humbly admit was what I thought and did at that time. Alternatively, I could have remained open to the message and gone looking for a Smoky Quartz crystal.

Ironically, months after I returned home, I noticed that I already owned several Smokys which I had purchased years before because they were pretty! It turned out they were powerful energy conduits for me, sitting right there in my home being ignored.

Catch and Release

We all do things at times that are out of alignment with the Rays. Picture yourselves as a spinning top that is in perfect alignment and smoothly spinning. Then a hitch happens within us caused by fear, which manifests as a thought, an action, words, or being drawn into another's drama. The top jumps erratically, causing it to stop spinning and fall over.

Catch this moment and note what happened. Aha! Resolve to fix it, if needed, or feed it the Ray of acceptance to dissolve the energy of it. Imagine the top sits quietly on its side or perhaps gets up but reverses its spin while we assimilate, release and repair to refocus on holding our Light. The Light then spins the top forward again in balance.

I remember a time when I resolved to stop talking about myself in a negative context. We all do it. A friend says we look lovely and we put a hand to our head and say "oh, thanks, but I couldn't do much with my hair this morning" instead of just being grateful. I voiced the intention to stop immediately. In reality, it is more like a catch and release.

Breaking habits is not always instant. So, I would catch myself, judge myself for breaking my intention, sort through why I am judging myself, forgive myself, release the emotions of failure and judgment, recommit, and carry on.

The good news is that eventually this cycle slows down and ceases altogether. The energy of the voiced intention eventually dissolves the action until the action's pattern dissolves into nothing.

Focus Your Choices

Keeping the Light means making all our choices from the Light. It means choosing Love over fear all the time. It involves filtering even simple everyday choices through the Rays. Focusing can be tricky. The way to amplify something is to focus on it. The way to decrease something is to focus on its antidote rather than putting "do not" in front of it. Let us say that I am trying never to judge myself. I will think, "Do not judge yourself, Catherine." Perhaps I will meditate on these words or create a personal mantra.

The fact is that by repeating any phrase containing the word judgment, I am actually cementing my focus on judgment. As an antidote, "love me" is what comes to mind, though this word is not always that helpful, as we have seen in the previous chapters. More correctly, I am looking for, "accept yourself."

To fully release self-judgment, I need only conjure up what it feels like in all my senses when I have the acceptance Ray of Light beaming strongly within me. Everything created within is experienced without. There is a sensation in my diamond core when I have connected my personal will with my Soul and lifted my shoulders to bear this acceptance fully, and I believe it in my heart. I memorize this sensation and focus on it.

There is a beloved tale, often repeated because it is so beautifully simple and profound. Honoring the Cherokee, I summarize it briefly. Grandfather is sitting with his young grandson by the evening fire. Questions have been posed by the young one of his inner conflicts. Grandfather replies with the story of two wolves battling. One carries anger, jealousy, greed, resentment, inferiority, lies, ego. The other brings joy, truth, love, hope, humility, kindness, compassion, empathy. These represent the human battle within each of us.

The boy asks which of the wolves will win. Grandfather quietly responds, "the one you feed."

When we feed one, the other transforms and vanishes.

Power Up Your Intent

Power comes from clarity. The world is as it is because of what we intend it to be. We need to be very clear in our purpose. Intention sets the laws of Spirit in motion. Without a conscious statement of intent, there is a vacuum. Into this void will filter our subconscious thoughts.

Unconscious intentions rather than conscious intentions can be dangerous, creating a chaotic spinning of events around us. For a day or a week, choose to believe that we conjure what we think. Experiment with this and note what happens.

Here is a funny example of the power of intention. I was sitting idly one day on my meditation mat and decided to focus on the various energy centers around and outside of me—the stellar gateway, the soul star, the causal, the earth star. All was fine until I focused on the causal, which is located behind our heads. My intent was focused so firmly that the third eye area of my forehead and my cheeks and nose started to invert itself.

The muscles were literally trying to turn inwards towards the back of my head where that center resides. It was excruciating, to say the least.

It took me a while to uncramp, and then I had a good laugh at myself. My intent was a little off the mark. I was unconsciously tuned to the physical rather than the energetic and was so focused that my face was attempting to do as I asked!

I heard a story long ago, which has stuck in my memory, which illustrates the power of intent. Two celibate priests were savoring a rich cup of espresso at a café on a sunny plaza. One was younger, the other more seasoned in years and in life. The older priest was openly admiring the beauty of the women passing by, and not being shy about sharing his thoughts aloud.

The young priest did not understand the older man's lively interest in the women, and he questioned this in a dogmatic, self-righteous way. The elder priest laughed and explained that to be a priest was to hold the intent to be celibate, not to renounce his ability to appreciate beauty. It was natural to admire this beautiful creation called woman, without changing his choice to honor his intention.

Once we have stated an intention, we know the right choices to make to hold this intent. Each time we deny these right choices, we drain our life force, our personal power, and veil our Light. This can apply to even the most seemingly insignificant decisions, like stating the intent not to eat sugar for a week. The strength of our intention comes from what we most often view as small or insignificant things.

If we can be impeccable in our "little" intentions, then we can trust ourselves with the "big" ones. I always ask myself about how I am feeding my intentions. Have I slipped up? Have I lost the focus of the Rays in my intentions?

This Light feeds our bodies as well as our Souls. Covering this Light or flipping it open and closed erratically can lead to significant imbalances in the long term.

Practice Discernment

I think one of the hardest lessons for us is to discern when it is best for all that we walk away. We are taught from a young age to turn the other cheek, in the sense of forgiveness of another's actions towards us. I believe this saying also can mean, turn the other cheek as you walk away.

We are to live in and share our Light and Love. Yet I have also come to believe that we are not expected to voluntarily place ourselves in situations that tax our human limits beyond our control. We each have unique capacities to handle the variety of conditions life throws at us. I believe that we are never given more than we can handle.

I also believe that sometimes we place ourselves in situations that we are not supposed to be in. I also believe that our capacity to handle situations changes regularly. What may be too much on one day might be just fine on another. When we are in tune with our Soul and fully alive in our

Light, we will have clear discernment of when to stay in a situation and when to leave. Where we are guided to be, we will be given the required personal resources.

An example of this happened as I was writing the section on nurturing our Light. I had a recurrence of severe angina-like pain. It had been decades since my heart attack, yet my first thought was heart – hospital! However, I stopped and took some time to commune with my Soul, and it told me that I was calling forth remnant cellular pain memory. Earlier that week I had received a clear message from my Soul that I was to avoid a particular event, as it would be tricky for me to navigate and it was not really necessary for anyone that I be there. It was more important that I continue writing and guard my energy.

I ignored that message. Consequently, I ended up in a five-day-long situation that was crossing the limits of my personal boundaries, as they were at that time. While I was able to remain heart-centered, the effort it took to do so resulted in cellular memory of similar times from long in the past when I was not able to stay heart-centered. I was inflicting this on myself and paying the price with pain. It was an extreme example of how the energies of our thoughts and actions exhibit in our physical bodies. Ironically, I was trying to put into words the concept of nurturing our Light and I had mindlessly stepped into a situation where the opposite occurred!

Stabilize

Our Light is made stable by never giving the power of it away. There is a story of devout monks torn from their land and incarcerated for decades in a foreign prison. Upon liberation, one monk was heard to say he had almost died. He did not mean physical death, although perhaps it would have led him there. He meant that he had nearly succumbed to hatred. Hatred would have killed his Light, which to him would have meant death to his Soul.

In other words, he almost lost the stability of his Light. By turning to hate, the monk would have extinguished his Love and given his power to those whom he had decided to hate.

One of the gravest mistakes we make is to give away the power of our Light to others. Often this is to those we mistakenly believe have Light that we do not. Believing it exists outside and in others is like giving it away. Think how much of our current life is focused on worship. We worship Hollywood stars, royals, intellectuals, inventors, politicians, billionaires, practically anyone that has made it into the spotlight.

When we worship another, we send our power out of ourselves. This invests our energies in another and may actually close our hearts to ourselves. This de-stabilizes our core. Our Light dims.

Our human structure is based on the principle of balance. It will work to rebalance itself whenever it feels unstable. It will go looking for energy to fill what has been taken away. If we continue to search for this Light outside of ourselves, stability will never be achieved. There is also the danger of others who are unstable searching to pull Light from us. A vampire, in energy terms, is one who sucks the Light from others to fill their own perceived void.

In this de-stabilized state, we have a constant see-saw effect within our energy field, which affects our moods, our mental functions, and ultimately, our body functions. When our connection to our Light source is active, we do not need to take any from others. Our Light radiates all around us, and nothing harmful can penetrate through it unless we allow it. In other words, we will not take energy from others, as there is no lack of our own.

We exude this Light to all that come within a close radius of us. Sometimes this is a passive function. You may have noticed this when someone asks you simply to show up somewhere. No need to do anything, just be there. It spreads to others without us realizing it. At other times we direct this Light actively, as healers or teachers, guides or mentors.

The Light pierces like a sword to the heart of a person. In an instant, it can transform and transmute, and not everyone is comfortable with that process for themselves.

Like a moth to a flame, many are attracted to this Light. Their Soul wants to live in this Light and return to a place of balance. How can anyone genuinely revile you for acting from the Rays, from a place of wonder, respect, purity, benevolence, integrity, impeccability or honesty? If they do, know that they are attacking the Light in you, not you.

More often, though, the Light inspires others to move from fear into love.

We are All Lightkeepers

We are all Lightkeepers. We are the Light. We are all of equal Light. We are all one in the Light.

We are one with our Soul. We are one with the matrix beyond our Soul and beyond our Earth.

We are one with the Source through our Light. Our Soul is continually nudging us to live in our Light. We are to tend the Light, fan the flame, light the spark, and illuminate the path.

The Light breeds contentment, fosters joy, produces laughter before tears, compassion before hatred, empathy before cruelty. It eradicates the fear in the world by merely shining strongly upon it.

Nourished and supported, the Light will grow steadily. Fear cannot take root, and we will leave our physical bodies when they have run their course knowing we have truly lived the image of the Source's delight.

Stay centered in the Light of this Perfect Love for Love's sake. There is no need to do anything else but be present in love at each moment. Be at peace in the Light to inspire others to unlock theirs. Look into the heart of all things. In the most broken there is beauty searching for its Light.

The way of Light weaves all together. Single,

individual threads formed of different textures and colors become one congruent tapestry of exquisite beauty. In this understanding lies our path home to liberation.

11

Liberation

Liberation is a wide-open portal for our Soul's Light.

To be free means being spiritually awake and open to exploring, to explore all imaginings, without boxes, labels, inflexible dogmas. To be whole means the Soul and human are in harmony. There are many examples of those who receive all the material wealth they can imagine and still cannot find serenity. Others diligently explore every nuance of scientific, psychological, and philosophical thought, and still cannot find peace. Still, others endure through their days wondering what is happening to them.

Liberation is the slaying of ignorance.

The transcending of willful blindness. No lies, no dominance, no enslavement. There is no danger in changing or flipping our perspective — no monsters under the bed. Human life has finite layers of richness. Soul Light adds layers luxurious in infinite wisdom and knowledge. Light brings us out of fear and opens us to wisdom, grace, freedom, and joy.

Liberation is knowing our Light is already perfect.

We do not need to strive for perfection, as our Soul is already there. We need to strive to connect with our Soul and live in its Light. Perfection is one of those concepts that flow from our three-dimensional polarities. Something is perfect only in comparison to something else. Perfection on Earth comes as we are aligned and connected to our Source through our Soul and we allow free expression of its Light in our human experiences.

Liberation is the power within—knowing that we alone can save our self from our self.

This is transcendence. No one else can save us. We save ourselves through activating our Light, the power that comes directly from our Source, through the conduit of our Soul. We perpetuate the energy of separation when we think of the Source Light as outside of us, something we must search for out there in the world to bring back within. We do not reject the external world. We see the reality of the space it occupies by understanding that we are more than a human being. We are a Soul-human being.

Liberation is the wild, primal force that dwells in our deepest places.

Too long has it been forced to bend to externally-imposed rules. It is a visceral force. One to be felt throughout our senses. One to be respected as dwelling in all of us. Understand that the Light carries no restrictions. Instead, when you live in its Rays, all that primal wild creative force breaks free. It is not a tame force. It roils like a stormy sea; it shines like a brilliant sunrise, it blows with the strength of a hurricane and yet rocks us gently and burns like the embers of a well-tended fire.

Light is our birthright. It comes from our Source to form our world and sustain the Earth. It is our right to do whatever it takes to dig deep and find it dwelling within our hearts. To ask for and receive more. To unleash its full power in our lives.

It is our nature to spin and sing and laugh and to revel in our ability to experience the richness that is ours. To walk the shores of crashing surf and cry real tears from the power of it, to soar our inner planes with the eagles, or quietly place a blessing on the brow of a tiny babe of Light.

It is our calling to fully express what we are through the Light of the Source's Perfect Love. Such a joyful release; shine with wonder, respect, benevolence, purity, impeccability, integrity and honesty, always and forever.

Liberation. Truth. Grace.

In the darkest hour of the night, I sat high on the edge of a mesa plateau. I was deep in meditation suspended between the red earth and the crystalline stars. I was at peace with the world and with myself; in harmony with the warm, night breezes and the small rustlings of nocturnal creatures. Content.

Suddenly, a figure appeared in front of me, seated in a mirror image of myself. He was ancient and weathered, yet fiercely focused and intent. He was a medicine man of old, wise, withered in body, yet fiery of spirit and passionate with wisdom.

He locked his eyes to mine. Instantly my vision shrank until all I could see were his two eyes. Then he locked his third eye with my third eye. It was as if we were tethered for eternity, unable to move, or blink, or think.

It was the strangest feeling I had ever had, yet I was not afraid. Instead, every sense was heightened, waiting for something momentous to occur. And it did.

My inner vision expanded as if I were viewing the entire universe. I shapeshifted through him to become a tiny creature light enough to travel on the back of a bird. For balanced on the wise man's arm was a magnificent eagle beckoning to me.

We flew out over the land, so high I could not distinguish anything below except a blanket of darkness. Somehow the man's hand was in my sight guiding me to look one way and the other, opening up the blackness.

There were scenes of such grief and horror; it was as if the very earth were groaning under the weight of the terrible anguish of its children. I cried out! Surely there is a way forward, out of this path of fear and destruction.

The sage's eyes glowed even more fiercely, and my third eye truly began to ache. Eagle flew me closer to the ground. The darkness appeared like a never-ending shroud, but he bid me look closer for there was something else there.

At first, I saw what looked like tiny sparks that sputtered and blew out. Then they began mixing together and glimmering like small lamps. Then more and more would merge, and the lamplight became broader and brighter.

Eagle flew me away, higher and higher. This time I could still see these glowing pools of light scattered in the blackness. I saw that there were many of them. Some quite small, others more significant and growing.

The faces of the world's tormenters came flying at me. I saw them parade before me like a kaleidoscope. A voice tolled like a bell. They would not succeed in snuffing the Light from this world. I waived them onwards. I commanded them to return from whence they came. Their time had passed. Many of them have come, and all have gone.

Gradually the two eyes of the ancient one came back into focus. His smile emanated such beauty, wonder, and joy, reflecting all the Light shining up from the Earth below.

He said, very simply: "Feed the Light."

Instantly, I was back in my body. As he faded away, I heard Eagle whisper:

"You know."

In Gratitude

To my daughter Rachel: you have been a sparkle of Light to me since the moment you were conceived.

To my husband Gilles: your love has uplifted me through so many Earth walks.

To Karen Stuth, owner of Satiama Publishing: your unwavering heart is a blessing to the world.

To my family and friends: your rays of Light dance around me in exquisite colors.

To all Lightkeepers: may we glow as a thousand brilliant lamps at midnight.

Catherine Grace Landry

About the Author

Catherine Grace Landry is an award-winning author, teacher, speaker and spiritual guide. She is a qualified shamanic practitioner, crystal energy therapist and Kundalini yoga instructor. She lives in Ottawa, Canada. Follow her on Facebook, *The Way of the Simple Soul* page, and on her website www.catherinegracelandry.com. She can be reached at catherine@catherinegracelandry.com. *The Way of the Lightkeeper* is her second book.

Also by Catherine Grace Landry

The Way of the Lightkeeper and its predecessor, *The Way of the Simple Soul*, are the first two books in *The Way* trilogy.

The trilogy chronicles our human journey to connect to our Soul where we access the Essence of our Source, then to channel that Essence to our hearts for our personal liberation, and finally to pour out the grace of that Essence to all around us, for infinite serenity and peace.

The Way of the Simple Soul is the journey to discover and permanently incorporate our Soul's voice into the very fabric of our being, cementing within us the essence of joy.

The Way of the Lightkeeper take us to the deepest recesses of our being to open the portal of our heart's connection with Source through our Soul, embedding within us the Light/Love that is our liberation.

The Way of the Grace-filled Heart returns us to our earthly experience, where the path of Light/Love flows from Source, to us, from us to all around us, and then back along this loop, such that there is a continuous uninterrupted flow of grace and truth in our world. This book is scheduled for release in 2020.

www.catherinegracelandry.com